MATH

Facing an
American
Phobia

MATH

Facing an American Phobia

MARILYN BURNS

Math Solutions Publications

Marilyn Burns Education Associates
150 Gate 5 Road, Suite 101
Sausalito, CA 94965

Library of Congress Cataloging-in-Publication Data

Burns, Marilyn, date.
    Math : facing an American phobia / by Marilyn Burns.
      p. cm.
    ISBN 0-941355-19-5 (pbk.)
      1. Mathematics—Study and teaching (Elementary)   2. Math anxiety.
  I. Title.
    QA135.5.B839754   1998
    372.7'2—dc21   97-45225
                                                    CIP

Editor: Toby Gordon
Copy editor: Alan Huisman

Production: Alan Huisman
Book design: Jenny Greenleaf
Illustrations: Joni Doherty
Cover design: Barbara Werden

Composition: Cape Cod Compositors

Printed in the United States of America

05   04   03   02   6   7   8   9   10

To my mother,
Clara Meinhardt,

who can add a column of numbers
faster than anyone I know.

Contents

Acknowledgments viii

Introduction ix

1 Talking Turkey About Arithmetic 1

2 The Pizza Problem 15

3 Who Needs Tip Tables? 25

4 A Cupful of Fractions 37

5 Math Under Pressure 45

6 Calculators—Crutch or Tool? 55

7 Making Math Make Sense 65

8 School Math Then, School Math Now 75

9 Teaching Addition and Subtraction 81

10 Teaching Fractions 97

11 Teaching Percents 115

12 A Message to Parents 133

13 Solving the Phobia Problem 139

Not Your Everyday Answer Key 147

Acknowledgments

I'm deeply appreciative for all of the help I received while writing this book. I offer my thanks to:

Jeffrey Sellon and Toby Gordon for reading the chapters as I wrote them and thinking hard about how to make them better;

Nicholas Branca, Ann Dominick, and Sandra Nye for giving the manuscript a hard look from their teacher perspectives;

Alan Huisman for his caring and careful editing.

Introduction

This book tackles a subject that a disturbingly large percentage of the American population fears and loathes—mathematics. Math is right up there with snakes, public speaking, and heights. By far, it's the least favorite of the three Rs of education, and learning mathematics comes with its own myths.

"Only some people are good in math."

"You're only good in math if you have the math gene."

"People who are good in math wear thick eyeglasses and plastic pocket protectors."

"Mathematicians are different from most of the population."

"Face it, people who like math are nerds."

Otherwise well educated adults, confident and successful in most aspects of their lives, make easy confessions at dinner tables.

"I'm not any good in math."

"I never was any good in math."

"I hate math."

Math phobia is a widespread national problem. The negative attitudes and beliefs that people hold about mathematics have seriously limited them, both in their daily lives and in their long-term options. This situation shouldn't exist, and it doesn't have to. *Math: Facing an American Phobia* looks at why mathematics, a subject so important to our lives, has the dreadful reputation it does. It delivers a positive message about what math can and should mean to all of us and how we can help keep our children from adopting the negative attitudes many of us have.

The first book I ever wrote, almost twenty-five years ago, was for children. Titled *The I Hate Mathematics! Book*, it eases children into mathematics through games, puzzles, explorations, and—what many children love best—riddles. *Math: Facing an American Phobia* is for adults who were children when I wrote *The I Hate Mathematics! Book* and who realize that in some way, probably in many ways, mathematics is important. Many now have children of their own. And like all parents, they want better for their children, which means wanting their children to do well in school in all subjects, including math. Maybe especially in math.

The main premise of this book is that what was good enough for us in learning mathematics is not good enough for our children. Despite the reality that learning math was a bust for so many of us, we have pressed on with ineffective teaching approaches that clearly don't work. If they did, math phobia wouldn't be rampant today.

Even in the face of widespread failure in learning mathematics, we seem to want to cling to educational methods with a nostalgia for them that has long outlasted their usefulness and has perpetuated failure. The way we've traditionally been taught mathematics has created a recurring cycle of math phobia, generation to generation, that has been difficult to break. We start young children with counting and move them along through arithmetic, then on to algebra, geometry, trigonometry, and so on. The "and so on" depends on whether or not the student sticks with math, which means not falling off the ladder of math progress in school. But an alarming percentage of the people in our country have fallen off the ladder and feel like mathematical failures. And once people fall off the ladder, there seems to be no way for them to get back on.

Employers in all fields of work have issued the same request across the country: send us employees who can think, reason, and solve problems. The cry is loud and the call is reasonable. Children must be helped to learn mathematics in a better way than we were, so that mathematical limits do not shut them out of certain life choices and career options.

While reading this book, you'll have the chance from time to time to learn some mathematics. The math teacher in me couldn't resist sneaking in problems here and there to encourage you to get involved with mathematics—the familiar learn-by-doing approach. (Relax: I've provided an answer key in case you need bailing out.) But learning mathematics is not the main goal of this book, and reading it will not make you a math genius. Reading this book can, however, be your first step toward facing your own math phobia and helping others—children, family, friends— face theirs.

Talking Turkey About Arithmetic

CHAPTER 1

Thanksgiving is the one time of year in our country when we face a common math problem. It's actually an arithmetic problem. And although not everyone has to solve it, many people have a stake in its being solved correctly.

Let me be more specific. If you've ever been responsible for preparing the Thanksgiving turkey, you've had firsthand experience with this arithmetical dilemma: what time should I get up in the morning and start preparing the turkey so that Thanksgiving dinner is ready on time?

The Thanksgiving turkey problem is one of our nation's evident reasons for doing arithmetic. Thanksgiving is an important time, a time for families to gather, give thanks, and enjoy a meal together. It's a big occasion, and everyone wants it to be nice. That means, in part, that the food should be good. Dry white meat is a disappointment. Pink dark meat is worrisome. That's why I said that more people have a stake in the problem than just the person trying to solve it. Everyone who plans to join in the meal cares. Really cares. So maybe they should help solve the problem.

The arithmetic skills called for in this project are numerous. First, the cook has to decide what size turkey to buy. Cookbooks advise one pound of turkey per person, so the decision depends on how many people will be eating, right? But how much turkey do you figure for children? for leftovers? Also, Cousin Alan hasn't decided yet whether he'll come to your house or have Thanksgiving dinner with his wife's family in Pennsylvania. Aunt Betty and Uncle Jack have talked about flying in, but they're having trouble getting airline reservations. And if your daughter's college friend finds out that her parents won't be returning from their overseas business trip in time for Thanksgiving, she'll join you and your family.

So there's some uncertainty and variability involved in deciding the size of the turkey. That's no surprise. All real-life arithmetic problems have elements of uncertainty and variability. (What we were told in school about arithmetic problems being cut and dried isn't so, not by a long shot.)

Okay, you finally decide that a 16-pound turkey will do fine. And you decide to place an order for a fresh turkey at the market to be sure you'll have what you want.

"I'd like to order a 16-pound turkey for Thanksgiving," you tell the butcher. The butcher gets out the order book.

"Do you want a hen or a tom?" he asks.

When you don't respond immediately, he explains, "Hens go up to 16 pounds and toms start at 16 pounds."

"Either one," you say, "as long as it's 16 pounds."

"I need a range," he says then. "Do you want me to put down '14 to 16 pounds' or '16 to 18 pounds'?" Turkeys don't know about exact weights.

You're feeling weak. You stop a minute. Will Alan go to Pennsylvania or not? Will Aunt Betty and Uncle Jack be able to come? Will your daughter's friend's parents come home in time? Better safe than sorry. "Sixteen to 18," you say.

"Okay, a tom," he answers.

Phew, that's over. Now you go off to find the aisle that has what you need to make the stuffing. Packages of seasoned bread cubes make preparing stuffing easy. "Enough to stuff an 8-pound bird," the package says. Two packages, you think. But then you wonder, What if the turkey is closer to 18 pounds? Will two packages be enough? Another decision. (What we were told in school about there being one right answer to arithmetic problems isn't always so, either.)

It's clear that solving the Thanksgiving turkey problem requires quite a few numerical decisions. Deciding how big a turkey to buy and how much stuffing to make is only the beginning. Keep the problem in mind: what time should I get up in the morning and start preparing the turkey so that Thanksgiving dinner is ready on time?

How long will it take to fix the stuffing and stuff the bird? We've all learned that the turkey can't be stuffed the night before, that it has to be done right before we pop the turkey into the oven. How long will the turkey take to roast? How much time will it take to carve the turkey and make the gravy? But those decisions can wait until you have the turkey in hand.

The big day arrives. You picked up the turkey the day before; it weighs 16 pounds, 10 ounces. Some cookbooks say it takes 20 minutes a pound to cook a stuffed turkey; others say it takes only 15 minutes a pound if the turkey is over 12 pounds. More choices. Cookbooks also advise that the turkey needs to rest for at least 15 minutes before being carved. (Ah, you can use that time to make the gravy.)

You attack the calculations. Here, again, there are choices. You can figure mentally. You can get out paper and pencil. You can use a calculator or computer. Those are the three methods we use to do arithmetic—in our head, with paper and pencil, or on a calculator or computer. The choice we make depends on various factors—the numbers involved, how accurate we need to be, the tools we have available. With turkey arithmetic, the numbers can be messy. Remember the weight of the turkey—16 pounds, 10 ounces. There's a partial pound involved. And are you going to cook it for 15 or 20 minutes a pound or split the difference?

And there's that all-important final decision, one that relies on the best of your human judgment as well as on your arithmetical calculations: what time should you get started preparing the turkey? There's no answer book for this problem. (But you can take comfort knowing there are several turkey hot lines available at Thanksgiving. Really. Check with your butcher. I wonder what it takes to get a job answering 911 calls for turkey emergencies. Maybe we should start a Hall of Fame for these people.)

Now, aren't you sorry this problem wasn't in the math books we all had when we were children, as one of the many word problems we had to solve? It would have gotten us involved. Helped us build our sense of responsibility about Thanksgiving. Given us much-needed arithmetic practice in a real and useful context.

I'm serious. A problem like this is a good idea. But I worry that the way word problems are generally presented would cut the punch out of this one. It would include all the needed information. There would be no real stake in finding the answer. It might read something like this:

> Mr. Barker bought a 16-pound turkey for Thanksgiving. It takes 15 minutes per pound to cook. Mr. Barker wants to have the turkey ready at 5 p.m. What time should he put the turkey in the oven?

Not only is there no motivation to get involved, this is the kind of oversimplification of life that doesn't wash. Kids would be neither fooled by it nor helped to learn what real-life arithmetic demands. Isn't Mr. Barker lucky? He bought a turkey that weighs exactly 16 pounds. I don't know where he shopped, but turkeys in my supermarket don't come in tidy weights. And he doesn't have to worry about stuffing, or letting the turkey rest before carving, or allowing time to make gravy. His problem is just the kind of sterile problem our textbooks fed us. They were meant to be real-life problems, but they fell far short. There was no uncertainty or variability in the numbers to use and there was always one right answer.

Could you imagine a problem without a right answer in one

of our math books? Unheard of! That's the thing about math, we were told. You always know if you're right or wrong. It's clear. Just check the answer book.

Remember what I said before: there's no answer book for this problem. Real-life turkey arithmetic is anything but cut and dried.

My theory is that the way we were all taught arithmetic is the reason for the invention of the pop-up turkey, the kind with the red button that pops up to let you know when the turkey is done. You give your family a window of several hours and put them on call to eat as soon as the button pops.

Maybe you should bring up the turkey problem one evening before Thanksgiving. Have a dry run. Get everyone in your family thinking about it. Fill in the time you'd like to eat Thanksgiving dinner (yet another choice) and use the 16-pound-10-ounce bird or whatever makes sense for your meal. It's an excellent way to make math part of your family life.

The Thanksgiving problem is a once-a-year occurrence. But there are lots of other arithmetic problems we face daily. When I address parent or community groups about the math teaching that we ought to be offering our children today, I usually ask people to identify situations in their lives—outside work—when they need to do some arithmetic. Think of situations, I say to them, that require you to add, subtract, multiply, or divide to get some information you need. Here's the list a recent group came up with:

Balancing the checkbook

Shopping for groceries

Tipping in restaurants

Doing home woodworking projects

Deciding how much wallpaper to buy

Deciding how much paint to buy

Keeping score when playing games

Measuring fertilizer for the lawn

Figuring out what time to leave for the movies

Cooking

Calculating gas mileage

Figuring discounted amounts when shopping

Converting money when traveling abroad

Figuring out how much carpet is needed for a room

Budgeting household expenses

Making change

Dividing a check at a restaurant

The lists differ from group to group, but this one is typical. And any such list is a more than adequate indication that doing arithmetic is a regular part of our lives. This certainly makes the case for teaching arithmetic in our schools. Schools are charged with preparing our children for their future, and schools should teach children arithmetic because arithmetic is a skill they will need in their daily lives.

Okay, it's clear that arithmetic is important. But we need to think about what we need in our lives and what we were taught in school. I told the group that generated the list above about the three methods we use when doing arithmetic calculations, the methods I described for the turkey problem—in our head, with paper and pencil, on a calculator or computer. I asked them to look at each task on the list and tell me which of these methods they most often used in the situation. When people had different opinions, I checked each option offered. (See figure 1.1.)

The people in this group figured mentally for eleven of the sixteen tasks listed. This was no surprise to me. Every time I do this exercise with a group, people report that they figure in their head for more than half of the situations on the list. But it was a surprise to some of those who were in the group. They hadn't thought

Mentally	Paper and Pencil	Calculator	Task
	X	X	Balancing the checkbook
X			Shopping for groceries
X			Tipping in restaurants
	X	X	Doing home woodworking projects
	X	X	Deciding how much wallpaper to buy
	X	X	Deciding how much paint to buy
X	X		Keeping score when playing games
X			Measuring fertilizer for the lawn
X			Figuring out what time to leave for the movies
X			Cooking
X	X	X	Calculating gas mileage
X			Figuring discounted amounts when shopping
X			Converting money when traveling abroad
	X	X	Figuring out how much carpet is needed for a room
	X	X	Budgeting household expenses
X			Making change
X			Dividing a check at a restaurant

FIG. 1.1

about arithmetic this way. After all, for most of us, our recollection of learning arithmetic is that we did a hefty number of pages of paper-and-pencil exercises and that there was little emphasis on calculating mentally except for memorizing times tables.

I then asked the group which tasks on the list required an accurate answer and for which tasks an estimate would most often do fine. (See figure 1.2.)

Estimates were fine in most of the situations on this list. Typically when I do this exercise with groups, however, the number of situations calling for accurate answers is the same as those in which estimates are okay.

People explained their reasons. When one man claimed that he figured his gas mileage accurately each time he filled the tank, another replied, "When I figure my gas mileage, I round the numbers. So if I drive 243.7 miles and put in 10.2 gallons of gas, I divide 240 by 10 and that's close enough for me."

About wallpaper, one woman explained that it's sold in rolls, and sometimes only in double or triple rolls. "You always have to up the amount," she said.

"You'd better buy extra," another person added. "If you have to go back for more, the bin might be empty. Then they have to get another dye lot, and you're in for trouble."

The discussion went on to other instances in which overestimating was better than underestimating. "When you're in the grocery store with only $20, you'd better overestimate on things you put in the basket," one man said. "It's embarrassing to be at the checkout with too much stuff and not enough cash."

Someone countered, "With fertilizer, you'd better underestimate. Too much and you can burn your lawn."

This exercise carries with it several important implications about people's current math difficulties. There are disturbing mismatches between how we were taught arithmetic in school and what the arithmetic that we need to do in our daily lives really calls for. These mismatches have done a great disservice to many people.

First of all, there's a mismatch between the heavy emphasis our schooling put on computing with paper and pencil and the

Accurate	Estimate	Task
X	X	Balancing the checkbook (There was noisy disagreement about this one!)
	X	Shopping for groceries
	X	Tipping in restaurants
X	X	Doing home woodworking projects
X	X	Deciding how much wallpaper to buy
X	X	Deciding how much paint to buy
X		Keeping score when playing games (One person confessed to using occasional estimates for his golf score.)
	X	Measuring fertilizer for the lawn
	X	Figuring out what time to leave for the movies
	X	Cooking (One person lobbied for accurate. You had best be accurate when baking, she said.)
X	X	Calculating gas mileage
	X	Figuring discounted amounts when shopping
X	X	Converting money when traveling abroad
	X	Figuring out how much carpet is needed for a room
X	X	Budgeting household expenses (You can never be exactly sure what you need, someone said, arguing that budgeting calls for estimates.)
X		Making change
X	X	Dividing a check at a restaurant

FIG. 1.2

real-life need we have for being able to calculate in our head. Since we solve more than half of the arithmetic situations we encounter by figuring mentally, our children should be given plenty of opportunity to learn to do arithmetic in their head.

Parents generally raise two questions about this issue. One is: shouldn't our children learn to compute with paper and pencil first before they learn to compute mentally? No, I answer, and it's an easy answer to explain. Computing has to do with thinking, not writing with paper and pencil. Requiring children to learn paper-and-pencil computation first is putting the cart before the horse. It's like expecting children to learn to write before they can tell their own stories. The thinking children do about numbers goes on in their head, and they're certainly able to think before they learn to write.

The other question that parents raise is: but don't you need to know how to compute with paper and pencil in order to know how to compute mentally? No, again. This question implies that the only way we compute is by using the paper-and-pencil methods we were taught, and that's not so. You'll read more about this in chapter 3 in relation to how we figure tips in restaurants. But for starters, right now, double 38 in your head. When I ask groups of students or adults to do this, I follow up by asking them to explain their method. Usually there are four or five different ways. (Ask some of your friends and see what methods they use.) Some people double 30 to get 60 and then add 16; some double 40 to get 80 and then subtract 4; some double 35 and add 6. Some calculate in their head the way they learned with paper and pencil, by "seeing" the problem on their mental chalkboard and then doing the computation. Using the standard school procedure is not the only way reported, and it is neither necessary nor typical.

Learning to compute with paper and pencil does not necessarily prepare children to compute mentally. Although paper-and-pencil procedures give children efficient ways to do computations, a danger is that children may learn to do them by rote rather than rely on reasoning. Yet reasoning numerically is essential in order to compute mentally. No one method for doing arithmetic in our head is useful in all situations. The method we use depends on the numbers we're dealing with, the context in which we encounter them, and the extent to which we need to be accurate.

By the time children leave elementary school, they should be able to do mental calculations with all numbers up to at least 100. Developing this proficiency requires practice. Yet more than 75 percent of the arithmetic instruction we received was spent on practice with paper and pencil. Little attention was given to mental computation. And while children should be able to figure with paper and pencil, what we've long needed is to provide a balance between learning to use paper and pencil and learning to calculate mentally. (More about both of these later.)

Second, there's a mismatch between the attention our schooling put on accurate answers and the real-life need we have to be able to estimate and know when estimates are appropriate. I remember as a child having textbook pages of arithmetic exercises with instructions that said: *Estimate first. Then figure.* No reason was evident to me for why I should estimate first. My papers were always judged on the correctness of my calculations. A wrong answer, even if close, was wrong.

I don't think there's anything wrong with demanding correct answers. But if that's the goal, why should I bother to make an estimate? The textbook rationale was that if you estimated, you would have a way to check whether your answer was reasonable. This rationale didn't convince me as a child, and it isn't convincing to children today. They're far too savvy for that kind of logic.

Missing from the schooling many of us had were opportunities to think about the appropriateness of estimates not as applied to isolated arithmetic exercises but in the context of situations. We didn't have opportunities to learn how to decide when an answer had to be accurate and when an estimate would do (or be even better). We didn't have to think about whether an overestimate or an underestimate would be more appropriate or if it wouldn't matter.

A steady diet of pencil-and-paper practice didn't give us the chance to see the purpose and usefulness of arithmetic in real life. We were able to be successful in arithmetic, even encouraged to be successful, by learning procedures by rote. Thinking and reasoning weren't required.

Of all of the situations on the earlier list, only checkbook calculations resemble textbook exercises, and only a few of the other situations involve firm numbers and call for exact answers. As with the turkey problem, most of our real-life arithmetic problems involve numbers that are uncertain or variable. Exchange rates change. Budgets require a contingency plan for surprises. We need to allow for the width of the blade when we measure where to cut a piece of wood. When we figure the tip in a restaurant, we round off the amount and factor in our judgment about the quality of the service.

Textbook word problems were another standard part of our elementary math instruction. When we were young, the word problems involved simple addition:

> Sally had 7 crayons and Jill had 5. How many did they have in all?

Then we moved on to subtraction:

> Bill had 9 candies. He gave 3 of them to friends. How many candies did Bill have for himself?

Sometimes we had a page with addition and subtraction problems all mixed together. Ask any teacher about these pages and you'll learn that they are trouble. "Is this a plus or a minus?" many children ask, not sure what to do. Practice with sums and differences isn't enough to prepare all children to know when to apply those skills, even in the simplest word problems. Word problems in the upper grades were more complex, requiring two or more steps:

> John went to the market and bought 5 pounds of apples. Apples cost 39 cents a pound. How much change did John get from a $5.00 bill?

In all of these examples, the goal was to use some or all of the numbers in the problem to arrive at the "right" answer. The problems took one or more steps; estimates weren't needed; ambiguity or messy numbers, as we encounter them in real life, weren't part of the experience. It's no wonder that so many people feel ill equipped to deal with the numerical problems we face today. Should I refinance my home? Is it better to have a fixed or a variable rate mortgage? How much do I pay in interest when I run up a balance on my credit card bill? What will the loan for my new car really cost? How can I plan so that I will be able to afford my children's college education? We've traditionally considered the "basics" of arithmetic as memorizing the facts and learning to do paper-and-pencil computations. Some people still hold to that notion. What was good enough for me is good enough for my kids, they say.

Not so. If what we experienced was good enough for us, then how come so many adults today admit to not liking mathematics, avoiding it, even being seriously math phobic?

The solution is not to make math easier or simpler. Quite the opposite. The change we need to make is to broaden the notion of what basic arithmetic is so that it includes the complexity of real-life arithmetic, so that it promotes the thinking and reasoning that are essential life skills. Memorizing facts and becoming proficient with computation are no longer sufficient minimal competencies. We need to ask more of our children and provide more rigor in their arithmetic instruction so that they will be prepared to face the numerical situations they encounter. And more rigor does not mean doing more of the same kind of problem or increasing the number of digits in an arithmetic exercise so that three-place addition becomes four-place addition, for example. More rigor means pushing students to apply the concepts and skills they've learned in new and different ways and challenging them to face more complex problem-solving situations.

The basics as we've known them must be broadened. Our children must be able to:

1. Recognize how to use arithmetic to solve problems in a variety of contexts.
2. Define the problem to be solved and identify the numbers and operations to be used.

3. Perform the calculations using one or more of the following methods:
   • in their head
   • with paper and pencil
   • on a calculator.
4. Evaluate the reasonableness of an answer and make a decision about what action to take.

A friend of mine is an interior decorator. "I was never good in math," she once told me. "I'm so grateful that I have work to do that doesn't rely on doing math."

I looked at her in amazement. To do her work, she has to measure the dimensions of rooms for floor covering and wallpaper, figure yardage for drapes and upholstery, calculate the cost of the goods, and prepare invoices for clients, figuring in the percentage for her service. I've watched Barbara size up rooms, her eyes darting as she takes in the floor area, the ceiling height, the placement of windows and doors; suggest the right amount, size, and scale of furniture; and prepare an estimate that is amazingly close to the actual cost. I experienced this firsthand when we remodeled our house. No math? What was she talking about?

I asked her.

"Oh, that," she said. "That's easy. It's those pages of math problems in the book I never could do."

There's the problem. People think that doing math in books is what doing math really is. It's not. What we need to do for our children is get math off the textbook and worksheet pages so they can see reasons for doing math and gain experience using math to solve problems. Our school instruction focusing primarily on performing calculations and using primarily paper and pencil to do so fell far short for many of us, and it doesn't provide our children the arithmetic instruction they need. We have to change our perception about what doing math is; we can begin by broadening our arithmetical scope.

The Pizza
Problem

I was going to call this chapter "Cooking, Geometry, and Measurement," but I worried that everyone would skip it. The title made the chapter seem dull, too dull even to write, and that's no way to try to make math more interesting and accessible.

This chapter was inspired by Rosie Daley's book *In the Kitchen with Rosie* (Knopf, 1994). You may know about this cookbook. It has fifty of Oprah Winfrey's favorite recipes created for her by Rosie. Anyone who has seen Oprah recently knows how terrific she looks. She's trim, looks beautiful, and obviously feels good. And she credits Rosie's cooking with helping. Oprah writes in the introduction of the book: "This new way of eating very low fat, low sugar, low salt (I like to call it 'clean eating') has made such a difference in my life. I feel better." And, as the photo on the book flap shows, Oprah is living proof of the healthy effects of Rosie's culinary talent.

I was ready. I bought the book and browsed through the recipes. I tried some of the salads and the "unfried" dishes. They're tasty. Then I got intrigued by the recipes for pizzas.

I never allow myself even to think about pizzas when I'm trying to lose weight, and here were recipes for three variations of individual 5½-inch pizzas that ranged from 190 to 232 calories.

And the toppings sounded delicious—one was a pesto pizza with mushrooms and olives, one was a goat cheese pizza with artichokes and onions, and the third was a mixed vegetable pizza with blue cheese.

Can you picture the size of a 5½-inch pizza? You can think of 6-inch pizzas and still be close enough for this story. Just think of a plate that is about the size of one of Rosie's individual pizzas. That's what I did, and I decided that I could easily make a meal out of a pizza that size. Well . . . maybe two of them.

There's a hitch to preparing Rosie's pizzas. You have to make the pizza dough yourself, and that's a bit labor and time intensive. (That's when it helps to have Rosie or someone in the kitchen rather than just you.) But okay, I thought, the recipe calls for making eight of the 5½-inch crusts, so I can freeze the extras. I'll go for it.

I mixed together the water and honey. I sprinkled the yeast on top. I set the mixture aside to wait for bubbles to appear on the surface. That would be about twenty minutes, Rosie noted. Meanwhile I measured the flour, semolina, and salt into my food processor. When I saw bubbles, I turned on the machine and slowly added the yeast mixture through the feed tube. After a few minutes, I had a dough ball. I followed the instructions and put one teaspoon of olive oil into a large bowl, then put in the dough ball and rolled it around to coat it with the oil. As instructed, I covered the bowl with a towel.

Next I was to wait for about one hour "until the dough has doubled in size." What does Rosie mean by "double in size"? I wondered. How would I measure one ball to see if it's twice as big as another? I wasn't sure.

I set the kitchen timer. Now I had a free hour to do something else before rolling out the dough into the 5½-inch crusts, and there were plenty of things that needed doing. But I began to think about this "double the size" instruction.

The ball of dough in the bowl was about the size of a softball, about four inches across. I wondered how big the ball was supposed to be after it had doubled in size. Was it supposed to be eight inches across, like a volleyball perhaps? Is a volleyball twice the size of a softball? It's about twice the distance across, I agree, but it seems much more than twice as big.

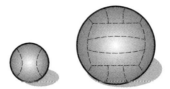

Of course, my math background is showing. Something triggered my math intuition. (That's what having a math background really means, that you have some math intuition.) My antennae were quivering. *Size* and *big* do not make clear what we are measuring.

I thought about a square. I got paper and pencil, sat down at the kitchen table, and drew a square.

A square isn't a ball of dough, I realize. It's not even a three-dimensional shape. But that's why I thought of it. I can draw a square more easily than I can draw a ball of dough, and I can see what I'd need to do to double the square's size. Should I double the length of its sides? I did that, drawing a square with sides twice as long as the sides on the first square I drew.

Whoa! The new square was four times the size of the first one, talking about its *area*, that is. The sides of the new square had each doubled, I could see, and the total distance around the new square, its *perimeter*, was twice the perimeter of the small square. So the perimeter had doubled while the area got four times bigger.

But I'd wanted to draw a square that was double the area, not four times the area. (Here's a math problem for you to try, if you'd like. Draw a square. Then try drawing a square that has twice the area. How do the lengths of the sides of the two squares compare? When you're ready, check the solution to problem 1 in the answer key.)

But I was really interested in doubling *volume*. I thought about a cube. I can draw that easily, and it's three-dimensional.

Okay, how will I double the volume of this cube? Maybe it will be a cube with its dimensions doubled. I sketched a cube with sides twice as long.

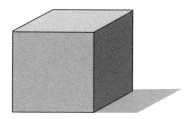

Yikes, it's really big. It would take four of the original cubes to build just the bottom layer of this larger cube, and then four more cubes for the top layer.

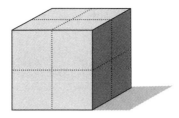

Now I have a cube with a volume eight times as big. I only wanted twice the volume.

Back to the ball of dough. Maybe I should start again, this time thinking about a circle. I sketched one.

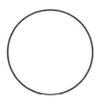

What would a circle look like that was double in size? Maybe I should double its diameter. I sketched a circle with a diameter twice as long.

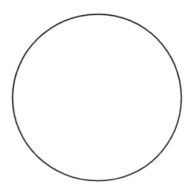

Hmmm, what happened appeared to be the same as what had happened when I doubled the sides of the square. It looked as if four of the original circles could fit into the new circle, making it four times in area even though the diameter was only twice as long. I couldn't tell this for sure because of the shape of circles, but that's what it seemed like.

I wondered about the distance around the circle, its *circumference*. When I doubled the length of the diameter, did I double its circumference? I couldn't tell merely by looking. There are formulas for figuring out this sort of thing, but having to memorize those formulas was just the kind of experience that has made many people math phobic. If you remember formulas for circles, understand them, and know how to use them, fine. Two that help me are $A = \pi r^2$ and $c = \pi d$. But if these aren't of use to you, don't worry. We can make sense in another way about what happens to the circumference when we double the diameter.

Were you worrying about the time and my pizza dough? I was. I checked the timer, and there was more than half an hour to go before the hour was up. I peeked into the bowl. The ball of dough was larger, but now I was completely confused about how large it was supposed to be when it was ready. But since not even half an hour had passed, I decided to give the dough more time. Besides, I was into thinking about this double stuff. I left my growing ball of dough and went back to thinking about the circles I had drawn and what happened to the circumference when I doubled the diameter.

I know, I thought, I'll measure the two circumferences with string. Measurements with string won't be exact, but they'll give me a sense of how the circumferences compare. I found string in a kitchen drawer and carefully laid it on the circumference of the first circle, then cut it to length. I did the same for the second circle. What do you think happened? (You may want to try this yourself. There's no substitute for firsthand experience.)

I'll tell you what happened to me. The longer string was just about double the length of the shorter string.

I confess. This is exactly what I expected. (Yeah, you may be thinking, easy for her to say now that she's done it. Well, I told you to try it yourself.) The circumference of a circle is like the perimeter of a square. You can think of both as fences. It's just that the square fence has four straight sides and the circle fence is just one curve. Double the fence and you get four times as much space inside. Think about doing that for a garden. (Putting something in a context can help.)

So, I thought, what about the ball of dough? What did Rosie mean? All of my thinking didn't shed light on how big Rosie thought the ball of dough should be. I decided to trust that waiting an hour would produce the volume I needed. While waiting for the kitchen timer to buzz, I read on in the recipe.

"Preheat the oven to 400 degrees," the recipe said. No problem. I'd do that as soon as the hour was up.

Next I read, "Remove the dough to a work surface that has been dusted with the cornmeal and roll out evenly to a thickness of about $\frac{1}{4}$ inch." (It's hard to get away from fractions in life.) In preparation, I measured the cornmeal onto a cutting board.

I then read the next sentence in the recipe. Prepare yourself for it. It stunned me. I was stopped in my tracks. Cold. Shocked. Speechless.

Ready? The sentence read, "Cut out eight $5\frac{1}{2}$-inch circles, using a sharp knife and a saucer of that circumference."

My heart was pounding. A saucer of that circumference? Circumference? Circumference is the distance around a circle. Rosie can't mean that. I went back to the kitchen table and picked up the piece of string I had used to measure the larger circle I had drawn earlier (see page 19). If you didn't check my measuring yourself before, you've got to do it now. My string duplicating the distance around that circle looked about 5 inches long. I measured the string, and I was right. It was just over 5 inches.

A circle with a $5\frac{1}{2}$-inch circumference is about the size of a Ritz cracker! And I thought Oprah was going to eat just one of the pizzas, maybe two. No wonder she lost all that weight. I was thinking $5\frac{1}{2}$ inches in diameter, like a regular saucer, not $5\frac{1}{2}$ inches in circumference.

But maybe Rosie really meant to make teensy pizzas, and Oprah gets to eat all eight of them. There are three toppings in the cookbook, so she gets to mix and match.

Nah, who has saucers that are 5½ inches in circumference, unless you're robbing your child's toy tea set? I looked back in the book. There's a photo of Rosie opposite the directions, but no pizzas, just Rosie stir-frying veggies in a wok. I turned the page. There's another photo, this one of Rosie and eggplant slices. I searched all of the photos in the book. No pizzas.

The buzzer went off. I took out the ball of dough. It wasn't even close to the size of a volleyball, but it was definitely bigger than when it started. And it definitely would make more than eight Ritz-cracker-size pizza crusts.

I sighed with relief. Rosie had made a small mathematical error. She really meant *diameter*, not *circumference*. I hadn't expected this imprecision from Rosie. It was her use of the 5½-inch measurement that fooled me. If Rosie was being that exact about the measurement for the pizza crust, then I expected her to be exact about what it was we were measuring.

I made the eight pizza crusts. They were all pretty close to 5½ inches in diameter and pretty close to a quarter-inch thick. And pretty close was good enough, as it is in many arithmetic problems. The pizzas were delicious.

So what's my point? Shortly after I had discovered Rosie's error, I was teaching a course to New York City teachers about how to teach math to children. I told them about Rosie and the pizzas.

"Diameter, circumference, what's the difference?" one teacher said.

We talked about the difference. I reviewed the vocabulary. I had them use their hands to show what they thought was a 5½-inch circle. Most showed a circle the size of a typical saucer. I had them imagine a length of string 5½ inches long and then imagine forming it into a circle. Then I asked what they remembered about pi. More vivid than their recollection that pi was about 3.14 or 3½, most remembered having to memorize the formulas and not understanding either where pi came from or what purpose it served. They only remembered doing textbook exercises, plugging in numbers to find out areas, circumferences, diameters, or radii.

I don't know what Rosie's math experiences have been or what her attitude is toward math. I do know that whoever edited the book didn't catch the error. (I wrote a letter about the mistake to the publisher and got a letter back saying it would be corrected in future printings.) And I also know that learning formulas without understanding why they work is the kind of shortsighted view of mathematical teaching that has contributed to making math the national phobia it has become.

It turns out that pi describes a unique relationship. If you measure the diameter—the distance across the circle through its center—of the Ritz-cracker circle on page 19, it measures approximately $1^3/_4$ inches. Remember that the circumference—the distance around—is about $5^1/_2$ inches. What's the result when you divide the circumference measurement by the diameter measurement?

I did this on a calculator, dividing 5.5 by 1.75. The result was 3.1428571, which is pretty darn close to the value of pi. So, for a Ritz-cracker circle, the circumference is just about pi times its diameter. This doesn't happen only for Ritz-cracker circles. The relationship holds for all circles. That's what pi is, the relationship of the circumference to the diameter of any circle. For every circle, the circumference is close to 3.14 times as large as the diameter, and that fact earned the number its own name.

I said "close to 3.14" because pi isn't exactly 3.14 or $3^1/_7$. It's not exactly any number that we can write as a fraction. It's one of those decimals that goes on and on forever with no discernible pattern in the digits. It's called an irrational number.

We first learn about pi in about the fifth grade. And at that age, most children aren't ready to think about irrational numbers. But they can measure with string, rulers, and tape measures and be helped to discover for themselves this relationship that exists in all circles. Not only is the exploration one that gives children practice with measuring and dividing, it also gives them the message that math involves studying relationships and that learning math is about making sense of these sorts of relationships. If we had been taught math with that approach, maybe math phobia wouldn't be so rampant.

And maybe Oprah, with her unique ability to help others face a myriad of problems, can take on math phobia on one of her shows. We need all the help we can get.

Who Needs Tip Tables?

CHAPTER 3

H ave you ever had this experience: all of a sudden you notice something that you hadn't noticed before or hadn't particularly paid attention to? It's not something terribly unusual, a UFO or anything like that. It's something that's been around and that you've always known existed, but now it seems to pop up everywhere.

This happened to me with tip tables. I'd seen them from time to time on counters near cash registers in bookstores and drugstores, maybe in stationery stores, too. Look at that, I'd say to myself, a table to figure out tips in restaurants. Boy, what will they think of next? Maybe I'd pick one up and glance at it, but without my glasses that wasn't very interesting. And I'd move on.

About the time I started thinking about writing this book, I began noticing tip tables more often. I'd see people in restaurants put on reading glasses when the check arrived and take out of their wallets what looked like a credit card. I'd watch them hold the card vertically and peer down at it. I'd recognize the gesture. They were scanning a tip table.

It got up close and personal at a ladies lunch with some

25

friends. We were splitting the bill among the six of us. The waiter had put the bill next to Judith.

"Add on the tip and let us know what we each should chip in," Arlene said.

Judith blanched, looked at me, and said, "You do it." (That's what you get when you're the math teacher in the bunch.)

"Wait, I can do it!" Sue said with confidence. She was sitting right next to Judith and confidently snatched the check from Judith's hands. Sue reached into her purse and then held up, with a triumphant flourish, you guessed it, a tip table.

"Which will it be?" she addressed the table. "Fifteen or 20 percent?"

Sue is a successful real estate agent. She deals with numbers all the time, pricing houses, monitoring mortgage rates, making bids, figuring her commissions. Some of those calculations are complicated, I realize, and I know Sue uses a calculator—a programmable calculator, actually. And I also know that she has good intuition about the numbers she works with on a regular basis. But for restaurant bills she uses a tip table. It blew my mind.

When I saw Sue after that lunch, I asked her about using a tip table. "With all the figuring you do, do you really need to rely on a tip table at a restaurant?" I asked.

"I'm just being lazy," she said, laughing. Then she added, "But it's quite a conversation piece. So many people have asked me where I bought it that I could have sold it plenty of times over. Maybe it would be a good client giveaway. Lots of people really do need it."

The next time I saw a stack of tip tables on a bookstore counter I bought one. They were in a box with a sign attached to promote them:

TIP TABLES
Newly Revised
Now 15% and 20%

No wonder Sue was so proud of her tip table. She had the latest version.

As a beginning teacher, I taught eighth graders for six years. Problems with percents were a standard part of the curriculum. I regularly taught the three kinds of percent problems, showed many examples of how to do each, and gave the students lots of practice with them.

Do you remember the three types of percent problems? I haven't taught eighth graders for many years, so they're not right at my fingertips. (I think this fading memory of the percent rules is true for most adults today.) But I can reconstruct them, and the easiest way for me to do so is to think about percents in some context. Maybe a real-life context, like shopping.

I was shopping at Macy's on a day when there was a 25 percent discount sale going on. I needed some knockaround clothes and was looking over a rack of sweatshirts. A woman shopping nearby had picked out a sweatshirt and was holding it up, looking at the price tag.

"Could you tell me now much this will cost after the discount?" she asked me.

"Sure," I replied. I looked at the tag. It said $19.95.

Then the math teacher side of me took over and I began to think how I might help her figure out the discounted price for herself. If she were one of my eighth-grade students, I'd start by asking her to tell me the problem she was trying to solve. And then I'd ask what ideas she had so far. If she had a way to start, I'd listen and guide. If not, I'd either offer a suggestion or model for her how I would get started. I might say, I think of 25 percent as one-fourth. And then I'd ask, Does that make sense to you? If she nodded, I'd ask her to explain why she thought it made sense. Then I'd talk about thinking that $19.95 was just about $20.00, so I would think about what was one-fourth of 20. And on and on.

I caught myself in time. This woman wanted to know how much the sweatshirt would cost with a discount. She wasn't signing up for Percents 101 with a stranger in Macy's. Get a grip, I said to myself. I quickly figured that one-fourth of 20 was 5, which meant about a $5.00 discount.

"It will be about $15.00 before tax," I said to the woman.

"Oh, thanks, that's great," she said, now happy.

I began to feel a little funny. Why did she ask me? Could she tell I could do the math? Do I look like a math person? What vibes am I giving out here? But then I looked around and saw that no one else was nearby. I happened to have been handy. I tried to relax.

But what does this tell us about the three kinds of percent problems? There are three quantities in percent problems—the percent, the original amount, and the final amount. In a percent problem, you get two of these quantities and you have to figure out the third. In Macy's, the woman had the original amount and the percent, and I figured out the final cost of the sweatshirt.

When I think about all the adults in our country who do not remember the rules for percent problems, I divide them into two groups. Group 1 includes those people who feel, when confronted with a percent problem, that they can figure it out. They can approximate a discounted sale price with no difficulty. When they go to the copier machine to make an enlargement or reduction of something, they can figure out what percent to use. Figuring tips in a restaurant is easy. These people have confidence. They have a can-do attitude toward math. To them, percents are no big deal. Percents are their friends. No sweaty palms. No problem. That's group 1.

In group 2 are all the people who do not have percent confidence. They're not convinced they can figure out a percent problem when they need to. Or, worse, they're convinced they can't do so. They may even be suffering from mathematics disorder. (You'll learn what mathematics disorder is in chapter 13.)

Back to tip tables. I find the new and improved tip table I bought a depressing statement about our national arithmetic prowess. That anyone needs a tip table to figure out a tip is a dismal commentary. Anyone with at least an eighth-grade education should be able to figure a 15 percent tip in his or her head, without paper and pencil, without a calculator, and with confidence and certainty. The same is true for figuring a 20 percent tip, which I think is actually easier. That there's a market for tip tables is an embarrassment.

Maybe tip tables are the result of a conspiracy by waitpersons to influence how much tip we leave. But waitpersons wouldn't have listed some of the recommendations offered on the new and improved tip table I bought. Whoever made the table did the arithmetic correctly, I'll allow, but the answers aren't always right. For example, take a check for $1.00, maybe for a cup of coffee. Let's suppose the service was okay, so you're going for the 15 percent range. How much tip would you leave?

Well, the tip table I bought recommended 15 cents! Give me a break. Who leaves a 15-cent tip? This is ridiculous. Just as ridiculous is the tip table recommendation for a 15 percent tip on a check of $27.00. What would you leave? The table says $4.05. Who is the person who has this unyielding and absurd approach to arithmetic? Probably Mrs. Schneiderman, my fifth-grade teacher, who made us play Around the World. (I tell you about that experience in chapter 5.)

All right, I'll be reasonable. The person who did the figuring knew you weren't going to leave $4.05. He or she decided it was best to provide the exact amount and then leave it to you to do an important part of solving the arithmetic problem—making a human decision about what to leave. But, really, shouldn't all adults be able to do the calculations in their head?

And there is another catch with this new and improved tip table. Maybe the service was good, even above average. Not outstanding, though. Definitely not special enough for that 20 percent tip. You search your soul and come up with 18 percent. Yes, 18 percent. Well, maybe a little bit less. No, 18 percent. You stick with that.

Now what do you do? The tip table only gives 15 percent and 20 percent. If you're in group 2, as I suspect you are because you even have a tip table, what are you going to do?

I find the very existence of tip tables a mathematical tragedy. All because eighth-grade math didn't take. Where did we go wrong? And why is the size of group 2 so much larger than the size of group 1? It's very upsetting.

When I travel on airplanes, I usually chat a bit with the person sitting next to me. Often, the conversation turns to, "So what do you do?" I answer, "I'm a math teacher." Boy, do I get an earful, most often about the person's personal math tragedy.

"It was my worst subject."

"I hated algebra. I had to take it twice. Who needs algebra, anyway?"

"I did so-so up through algebra, but then geometry did me in."

"I was always bad in math, and my mother wasn't any good in it either." (These people seem to think they inherited a bad math gene.)

Some relate specific experiences that have remained vivid. "I can still remember being sent to the board in fourth grade. That was awful! Horrible!"

"It was long division that I hated. I never got those columns of numbers right."

"I hated the pop quizzes where you had to answer ten questions really fast. They made me feel completely stupid."

"I quit taking math as soon as I could. Two years in high school was more than enough for me."

There are times, of course, when my seatmate doesn't have negative feelings about math. From time to time I'll hear, "I always liked math," or, "I was always good in math."

Such was the case on a recent flight I made to Seattle. The man was a Boeing engineer. I sighed with relief. "Most people tell me that they weren't very good at it," I responded, "or don't like it, or even worse, hate it."

"I hear a lot of that, too," he agreed.

Then I asked, "About what percent of our adult population do you think doesn't like mathematics, or doesn't feel any good at it, or would even confess to hating it?"

After a moment, he said, "Maybe 85, 90 percent." Then he asked, "So, what kind of math do you teach?"

"I try to help people—children and adults—see math as interesting, relevant, and doable," I answered. "I try and give them a successful experience with math."

"Well, according to what I've read," he said, "we aren't teaching right today. The kids in Japan do much better. We don't have rigor in our schools anymore. It's terrible that they let kids use calculators in school. That's ruining math teaching. I don't think schools expect enough from kids."

My heart sank. Here was a man who believed that the large majority of adults in our country are ill equipped mathematically and at the same time believed that school today isn't doing the job that it used to. How well did our schools teach if 85 to 90 percent of Americans are unsuccessful with mathematics? That's no record to brag about. Quite the opposite, it's evidence of the failure of what we were doing all along. And blaming it on the calculator? Oh, my. (For more about this, see chapter 6.)

But I was talking about percents, wasn't I. What's important to realize is that even group-1 people don't necessarily rely on the rules for percents. And they don't worry if they can't remember those rules. They know how to make sense out of situations that call for percents. They're confident in their ability to think and reason numerically.

But even if they do remember the rules for figuring percents, most likely they don't do what they were taught in school. They don't figure a restaurant tip by taking the total bill, changing the percent of the tip to a decimal, multiplying, then counting up the decimal places, inserting the decimal point, and coming up with the amount for the tip. They do something in their head. Maybe they figure 10 percent and add half again as much for 15 percent, or take 10 percent and double it for 20 percent. They may double the tax if they are in New York City, where it is a little more than 8 percent, or triple the tax if they are in Sheldon, Iowa, where it is 5 percent.

They do something appropriate to the situation. And their answer won't be exact. No one leaves tips like 15 cents or $4.05. You either round up or down, and which way you go doesn't depend on any arithmetic rule, or any other rule, but on your best judgment in the situation. Your answer is imprecise, but you can explain why it makes sense.

Now that's doing a percent problem, I say, knowing how to calculate to get a correct answer and also knowing how to interpret the answer so it makes sense in the context of the problem. And it's a far cry from those pages we did in eighth grade using paper and pencil to compute exact answers to percent problems. It's no wonder rule-bound math learning never took hold.

How do I recommend teaching percents? Chapter 11 specifically addresses this question. But as a preview, I don't recommend an instructional approach based on teaching rules. More is needed to help students learn to reason with percents. And the more that is needed is the very challenge we face today in teaching mathematics.

What might replace teaching rules? I'd present the students with ideas to think about and problems to solve. The tipping problem doesn't make sense, since tipping in restaurants isn't within the realm of experience of most eighth graders. But the copier problem would work.

Imagine giving students half a dozen copies of some image, each in a different size. Think of a simple image, maybe a square. One of the squares is the original and it measures about 5 inches on a side. Each of the other squares is a different size, some smaller and some larger. The problem for the students is to figure out the percentage that was punched into the copy machine to make each size.

I'd first ask students to discuss in small groups how to approach the problem. Students would then present their methods to the entire class and we'd all discuss which ones made sense, which ones didn't, and why. We'd also talk about which methods were more efficient. There would be conversation and demonstration. The students would be actively involved. And how would students know whether their answers were right? They could test them on a copy machine. They'd get verification from a real-world test, not by relying on an answer book.

On another day, we'd comb the daily newspaper and highlight every reference to a percent. Then we'd talk about what each meant. We might even learn something about current events. Why not? Why should math be isolated from the other things that are important to us?

We'd have discussions about strategies for calculating percents mentally. We'd talk about using 10 percent of an amount, which is easy to calculate, to figure out other percents, like 5 or 15 or 20 percent. We'd talk about examples where starting with 10 percent isn't the best approach, where thinking about 50 percent, also easy to calculate, is useful. I might suggest how 10 percent and 50 percent could be used together to figure 60 percent of something. This would all be hands-on-the-desktop math, with no paper and pencil, without a calculator or computer. Just conversation, playing with numbers, and taking on challenges— all focused on reasoning with percents.

What do I hope will be the outcome of these kinds of experiences? Students will learn to think and reason about percents in a variety of situations, will be flexible in their approaches, and will learn to choose a method that is appropriate to the situation. They'll realize when an answer doesn't make sense, when they need to check their calculation or consult me or a classmate. They'll approach percent problems with the notion that they are supposed to make sense of them, and they'll persist until their answers do make sense.

Would I ever teach the three types of percent problems? Just the three problems and the rules for solving them? No. Why would I do that? When we were in school, teaching rules wasn't an effective strategy for empowering students to become proficient with percents. Why as a teacher would I perpetuate a method that clearly isn't successful?

I don't mean to say I wouldn't show students how to do percent problems. I'd show the students many different ways, not just three ways. I don't want the game of school to be for students to figure out which type of problem it is and, therefore, which method to use. I wouldn't demand that students do the problems in one particular way. Do we all figure tips the same way? No, and it's not necessary that we do. What is necessary is that we all understand what we're doing and why. No they-told-us-to-do-it-this-way excuse for a wrong answer.

If we do things our own way, how will we know if we're right? Sometimes, we won't. Life has no answer book. I can calculate a percentage correctly to figure out payments on a home mortgage, but that doesn't tell me whether it's better to get a fixed or a variable rate loan. For that, I need to weigh other factors and bring to the calculation a broader view and deeper understanding.

In school, students need to be asked to think and reason at all times, not merely learn rules and practice them. If students can be successful in a lesson merely by repeating what they've memorized or learned by rote, then the lesson simply isn't good enough. We must expect and demand that students learn to understand procedures, not only perform them. When their learning is based on understanding, students won't be incapacitated if they forget a rule or a step in a rule. Only with understanding will students be prepared to apply rules correctly in new situations. And only then will the need for tip tables become extinct.

Here's your problem for this chapter. (You were hoping I'd left you off the hook? No way.) The cover of this book measures $5\frac{1}{2}$ inches by $8\frac{1}{4}$ inches. I drew a rectangle that size and reduced it on my copier machine. Then I reduced it again using the same percentage. And then I reduced it a third time, again using the same percentage. The rectangle below is the result. What percent reduction do you think I used? Could I have gotten the same-size rectangle with two equal reductions? two unequal reductions? Get a ruler and give this one a whirl. Check problem 2 in the answer key when you're ready.

A Cupful of Fractions

I'm enthusiastic about fractions. I think fractions are interesting. I'd like to shake the hand of the person who thought of the way we write them, with one number perched atop another. I'm fond of the names of the two numbers in a fraction. *Numerator. Denominator.* They both have rhythm. Kind of toe tapping, don't you think? And fun to say.

I guess you've noticed that I like fractions.

What's there to like? you may be wondering.

Well, what's not to like? Fractions are a part of life, not to be rejected or scorned, but to be accepted, dealt with, even admired. They can be useful and handy.

Of course I like some fractions more than others, but I like all of them well enough. Even improper fractions. I refuse to discriminate against improper fractions. I never knew what the fuss was when the numerator was larger than the denominator. And such a name! Improper, indeed. (I'm not a big fan of anthropomorphizing animals or numbers.) I would have called them larger-than-1 fractions and let them be when they popped up.

I know why some people aren't crazy about fractions. It's the way we were taught about them in school. First of all, when we began to study fractions, we were told that we had to give up a notion that we believed was possible, even useful. That notion was: your half is bigger than my half. Every kid has experienced this phenomenon when sharing something with a sibling or a friend. If one half couldn't be bigger than another, then why did we need the you-cut-and-the-other-person-chooses system for sharing?

In school, however, we learned that when you divide something into halves, the reason you have halves is because both pieces are the same size. That's what halves are, we were told, two equal parts (as long as they come from the same whole). And it's important for children to learn that.

But it's something that children need to be taught with care. After a good deal of experience thinking of halves as different sizes when sharing, now children hear that having different-size halves of the same thing doesn't wash in mathematics. This kind of discrepancy makes math confusing to children. It gives them the message that you can't always trust what you know. Or even worse, it makes math seem more like a sneaky collection of tricks rather than a way to think about, describe, and make sense of the world.

Here's what I remember learning about fractions after finding out that halves of things had to be the same size. When you add fractions, we were taught, you add across the tops, but the bottom stays the same. Same for subtraction. When you multiply, however, you multiply across the tops and across the bottoms. And when you divide, you turn the right hand fraction upside down, and then you multiply across the tops and bottoms.

There was more. Sometimes when you wanted to add or subtract fractions, the bottoms weren't the same. Then you had to multiply the top and bottom of a fraction by the same number to change it to another fraction so that the bottoms of all the fractions you had to add or subtract matched, and then it was okay. And sometimes when you had to multiply or divide, only one of the numbers was a fraction and the other was a regular number, like 2, 4, or 7. Then you had to make those regular numbers into fractions by using a 1 for the denominator—$\frac{2}{1}$, $\frac{4}{1}$, or $\frac{7}{1}$.

And there was even more. A fraction is improper when the top is larger than the bottom. You couldn't have an improper fraction. You had to change improper fractions to mixed numbers, which were a whole number and a fraction together. And you had to do this quickly. It seemed to be very important to do away with improper fractions as soon as possible. Except in certain circumstances, such as when you made a fraction out of a regular number by putting it over a denominator of 1 (like $\frac{2}{1}$, $\frac{4}{1}$, or $\frac{7}{1}$ as I mentioned above) or when you made a fraction from a mixed number so you could add, subtract, multiply, or divide. But handing in a paper with an improper fraction was not a good idea. It would get you a red mark, for sure.

Odd as is may seem, I was interested in all these fraction rules. I eventually figured out why they made sense. And now I have the kind of understanding that makes me feel secure that if I forget a rule, I'll be able to reason through what I need to do.

How come I was able to understand the rules? A combination of factors, I think. When I was growing up, there was no fear, avoidance, or dislike of math in my house, and therefore I didn't learn to be afraid of it. (My father was an accountant and my mother was a bookkeeper.) Also, I had experiences outside school that helped build my understanding of fractions. I took piano lessons and had learned about half, quarter, eighth, and sixteenth notes, and about 4/4, 2/4, 3/4, and 6/8 time. The sewing and woodworking projects I did demanded that I measure with a ruler or tape measure, and that also helped my understanding of halves, fourths, eighths, and sixteenths. Fractions were useful to me. I expected them to make sense and I also expected the rules for working with them to make sense. Attitude is a big part of learning, coupled with lots of experience. I fared well.

That's how I came to have the understanding and courage to write this book.

But the rules of fractions didn't make sense so easily for others in my classes. I saw many classmates struggle with fractions. They struggled not to understand the why behind the rules but merely to remember what to do so that they wouldn't be humiliated when they were called to the board to do a problem. To many of them, the rules seemed grounded not in logic but in magic or, even worse, trickery.

Remember "yours is not to question why, just invert and multiply"? A helpful ditty in a jam, perhaps, but a symptom of the kind of rule-bound teaching that was the mathematical downfall for many. I'd like to replace that with "do only what makes sense to you." And then give kids the kinds of experiences with fractions that can help them build the understanding that makes for real math power. These experiences should include talking about fractions as we really do in life, not focusing on oddball fractions like $\frac{9}{17}$ or $\frac{13}{33}$, but on the common fractions we use and where we use them. (If a tennis player made 9 out of 17 first serves, we'd say she made about half of them, not $\frac{9}{17}$. If I sold 13 of the 33 raffle tickets I had, I'd more likely say I sold more than a third or fewer than half of them, not $\frac{13}{33}$.) These experiences should also include giving children concrete materials that can help them get their hands on exploring fractional relationships. And they should include having discussions about fractions so that students can hear one another's ideas and have the chance to clarify and extend their own thinking.

Oops, I haven't yet gotten to fractions in the kitchen, which is where I was headed. Sorry. I'll come down off my soapbox and get back to the point.

Anyone who does any cooking from recipes deals with fractions. Standard measuring cups, for example, have marks on them to indicate how to measure fractions of a cup. There usually are two columns of fractions on a cup. On one side are $\frac{1}{4}$, $\frac{1}{2}$, and $\frac{3}{4}$. On the other side are $\frac{1}{3}$ and $\frac{2}{3}$. And there's a 1 by the top mark.

No big deal, right?

Sometimes when you're cooking, you need to double a recipe. So, if a recipe calls for ¾ cup of chicken broth and you're making twice as much, how much chicken broth do you need? Figure this out and then notice how you did so.

I recently asked this question in a talk I gave to the Rotary Club in my town. I was asked to speak because the Rotarians have a math tutoring program in our school and they were honoring the volunteers. So math was my topic.

When I asked how much chicken broth they would need if they doubled this recipe, several people immediately called out the correct answer, "One and a half cups."

"How did you get the answer?" I asked.

"I just knew it," one person said. There were some agreeing nods.

"I did it fast in my head," another said, "¾ and ¾ make %4, and that's 1½." There were more nods.

"I'd dump in ¾ of a cup of broth, and then another ¾ cup," someone said. "I wouldn't bother with the fractions." There was laughter. This was good. I was talking about math and people were smiling and chuckling.

"That solves the problem," I said. "But suppose we were cutting the recipe in half? How much is half of ¾ of a cup of broth?"

"That's easy," one man said, "it's ⅜."

"How did you get that?" I asked.

"I changed ¾ to %8," he responded, "so ⅜ is half of %8." Again, nods. No one volunteered another method. I'm not sure they all bought into this man's thinking, but no one reported not being sure or not understanding his reasoning. This was supposed to be a luncheon talk, not a math confessional.

I pushed on. "Let's think about a measuring cup," I said. I reminded them about the marks on a standard measuring cup—$\frac{1}{4}$, $\frac{1}{2}$, and $\frac{3}{4}$ on one side, $\frac{1}{3}$ and $\frac{2}{3}$ on the other side, a 1 at the top.

"Aha!" I said, "There's no $\frac{3}{8}$ mark on the cup. What would you do?"

"Just eyeball it," one woman suggested.

"How would you do that?" I asked.

"Three-eighths is less than $\frac{1}{2}$ and more than $\frac{1}{4}$. It's about $\frac{1}{3}$," she answered.

"Is $\frac{3}{8}$ more or less than $\frac{1}{3}$?" I asked.

The room was quiet now. No smiles. No laughter. This no longer seemed like fun. People had that suspicious look I've seen on students' faces when they're worrying that they'll be called on next. Their eyes had dulled and lowered. They weren't liking me so much anymore. The luncheon talk was deteriorating into a math quiz.

I decided to change the tempo. I did what I would do with a class of students. "Talk with your neighbors," I said. "First compare how you knew that half of $\frac{3}{4}$ is $\frac{3}{8}$. And then talk about how $\frac{3}{8}$ and $\frac{1}{3}$ compare."

Geez, this is a fifth-grade problem, maybe a sixth-grade problem, and here were adults squirming. Intelligent, funny, responsible members of my community were being brought to their knees by a fraction problem. The room remained quiet for a moment and then chatter broke out. It was safer to talk in small groups. I sighed with relief.

So, how are you doing with this $\frac{3}{8}$ and $\frac{1}{3}$ problem? Glad you weren't there at that luncheon? Hoping you'll never hear me give a talk? Or confident that you know which is larger, $\frac{1}{3}$ or $\frac{3}{8}$, and can explain why? Give it a try before you read on.

I called them back to attention. "So, what do you think?" I asked.

One man called out confidently, "Three-eighths is larger."

"How did you figure?" I asked.

"I changed them both to twenty-fourths," he began. Another man hissed but was shushed by the people around him. The first man continued his explanation. "I figured out that $\frac{3}{8}$ is $\frac{9}{24}$ and $\frac{1}{3}$ is $\frac{8}{24}$, so $\frac{3}{8}$ is a little larger, exactly $\frac{1}{24}$ more."

Everyone looked at me. Was I satisfied?

"Makes sense to me," I said. "Did anyone figure a different way?"

"I changed $\frac{1}{3}$ to $\frac{3}{9}$," a woman volunteered. "And I know that when you cut something into eight pieces, the pieces are larger than when you cut something into nine pieces. Eighths are bigger than ninths, so $\frac{3}{8}$ has to be bigger than $\frac{3}{9}$."

There were murmurs of regard from the group. People were impressed. They turned in their chairs to look at the woman who reported that idea.

"I did it a different way," a man boomed from the other side of the room. People turned toward him. They were interested. I was less important now. Fractions were taking over. This was good.

"I got the same answer, but I used percents," he said. "I know that $\frac{3}{4}$ is 75 percent and that $\frac{2}{3}$ is $66\frac{2}{3}$ percent. That means that half of 75 percent is more than half of $66\frac{2}{3}$ percent, so $\frac{3}{8}$ has to be more than $\frac{1}{3}$."

There were whistles of admiration.

"Any other approaches?" I asked. Everyone looked around, expectantly, seeming to hope for more. There were no other ideas.

"This is just the kind of class discussion that our children in school should be having about fractions," I said. "They should have problems to solve and then the chance to talk about the different ways to make sense of them. They should talk about their ideas, learn from one another, and always look for the sense in what they are doing."

I wasn't taught math in this way, nor were the Rotarians at that luncheon. We all shared the common experience of doing pages of exercises and being told to cover our papers with a protective cupped hand so others couldn't see what we were writing.

There was no collaboration in our math classes, no talk about different ways to solve a problem, no context for the problems we faced. No wonder so many of us wound up not only confused about why math procedures made sense but also disliking and fearing math.

Back to the kitchen. Doubling $\frac{3}{4}$ of a cup of broth should be automatic for all of us. We shouldn't have to do what we were taught in school, to line up $\frac{3}{4}$ under another $\frac{3}{4}$, get a sum of $\frac{6}{4}$ (eek, one of those improper fractions), divide to get $1\frac{2}{4}$ and then simplify to $1\frac{1}{2}$. We should just know that doubling $\frac{3}{4}$ of a cup gives $1\frac{1}{2}$ cups. It should be familiar to us from having had enough experience exploring fractions and thinking about how they work. Familiarity through experience is the key, not memorizing.

But, even more important, should we forget how much $\frac{3}{4}$ plus $\frac{3}{4}$ is, we ought to be able to figure it out in a way that makes sense to us. Even more than one way. And having that ability comes from being taught math so that understanding is emphasized, ideas are explored, alternate methods are encouraged, and the purpose for what we are doing is always evident.

Math Under Pressure

CHAPTER 5

I stopped at my local discount drugstore one day to pick up a few things. One was hand lotion. I looked for what I usually buy—Vaseline Brand Intensive Care Lotion, the kind in the green container, with aloe vera. I was in luck. It was on sale. In fact, there were two sizes on the shelf and both were on sale! Each size had a special offer. The 16-ounce size read:

60% MORE FREE

16 OZ. AT THE 10 OZ. PRICE

The 20-ounce size read:

33⅓% MORE FREE

20 OZ. AT THE 15 OZ. PRICE

Hmmm. I know that larger containers typically are better buys, but I wasn't sure with these two. The smaller container promised so much more—60 percent—while the larger container promised only 33⅓ percent more. That seemed like an awfully big difference.

I read the offers again. The 16-ounce size was being offered at the 10-ounce price. But there weren't any 10-ounce sizes on the shelf. The 20-ounce size was being offered at the 15-ounce price, but there weren't any of those, either. All the containers on the shelf, green or any other color Vaseline hand lotion, were 16 ounces or 20 ounces. Was this a math teacher's dream or a consumer's nightmare?

What to do? Follow my usual policy and buy the larger size? Take a chance on the smaller size and go for the larger percent? This was ridiculous. I have a college degree in mathematics and I should be able to make an informed decision. This is just arithmetic, after all.

I looked at the prices. The smaller, 16-ounce container cost $3.49. The larger, 20-ounce container cost $4.39. Okay, what did that tell me? The smaller container cost 90 cents less than the larger container, but that didn't necessarily mean it was the better buy. The price per ounce for each container is what I needed to know.

As I mentioned in chapter 1, there are three ways to do arithmetic calculations—in your head, with paper and pencil, or on a calculator or computer. I didn't have paper and pencil with me. I didn't have a calculator or computer, either. I had to use my head.

Let's see, I thought, 16 ounces cost $3.49 and 20 ounces cost $4.39. I've got to divide. Bleh. Messy numbers.

Say, how about trying to help me out here? Which one do you think is the better buy? And which method would you use to find out? (Check problem 3 in the answer key when you're ready.)

I looked at my watch. Oops, it was getting late. I had a 3:00 P.M. meeting at the office and it was almost 2:45. I didn't have time to think about this any longer. I had to get going.

So . . . I took one of each size to the cash register, paid for them, and raced to my meeting.

In defense of my being a mathematical quitter, my on-the-spot inability to figure mentally, remember that I was late. Which made me stressed. And we all know that being stressed negatively affects our ability to think clearly. I didn't allow myself to feel inadequate, as if I were failing or falling short in some mathematical way. That kind of thinking leads people to believe they are serious math washouts. And presto, they're on the way to developing mathematics phobia.

Relax, I said to myself, driving to the office. Cut yourself some slack here. Buying both containers is an indication of your true commitment to mathematics. It's a positive investment in your own mathematical pursuits. You can try the problem later, after you get home, in the comfort of your favorite chair, with a nice cup of tea, perhaps.

There's no compelling reason to solve most problems on the spot. Mathematicians sometimes work on the same problem for years before they arrive at a solution. Work on a math problem for years? You're skeptical about that, I sense. Well, it's so. Take Fermat's last theorem.

Pierre Fermat was a seventeenth-century French mathematician who made a huge contribution to the world of mathematics, but he left a mathematical mystery when he died.

The story goes like this. In the early 1600s, Fermat bought a copy of the then-new French translation of *Arithmetica*, a book written by a Greek, Diophantes, in the third century. In the book, Diophantes discusses the Pythagorean theorem—$x^2 + y^2 = z^2$. This theorem states the relationship that exists among the lengths of the three sides of any right triangle. For example, if two sides of a right triangle are three inches and four inches long, then the third side has to be five inches. That's because $3^2 + 4^2 = 5^2$. (To check that, remember that 3^2 is 3×3, which is 9; 4^2 is 4×4, which is 16; 5^2 is 5×5, which is 25; and $9 + 16 = 25$.) When three numbers work like 3, 4, and 5 do here, they make up a Pythagorean triple, and a triangle with sides in those lengths will always form a right triangle. Diophantes writes that 3, 4, and 5 aren't the only trio of whole numbers that fit the Pythagorean theorem, that in fact there are an infinite number of whole number Pythagorean triples, numbers that fit the formula $x^2 + y^2 = z^2$.

After reading this, Fermat noted in the margin of the book that he agreed there are an infinite number of solutions to $x^2 + y^2 = z^2$, but that if the exponent is larger than 2, no whole number solutions are possible. He added, "I have found a truly wonderful proof which this margin is too narrow to contain." (That's one thing that mathematicians do, put forth theorems and then set out to prove them.)

After Fermat died, his copy of Diophantes' book was discovered in his library and his note in the margin was publicized. It tantalized mathematicians and many worked to construct the proof, but no one succeeded. The theorem wasn't forgotten, however, and it's been referred to ever since in math books as Fermat's last theorem.

In 1995, Andrew Wiles, a British mathematician, presented a proof of the theorem. For Wiles, it was the end of a nine-year pursuit of a childhood dream; for the mathematics community, it was a triumph to celebrate. When I heard about the proof, I was thrilled, not because I was particularly intrigued with Fermat's last theorem, but because I was impressed by the intellectual conquest.

I'm not telling this story to argue that more than 350 years is a reasonable length of time to solve a math problem. I'm arguing in support of putting the emphasis in mathematical problem solving on thinking and reasoning, not on speed. Sure, we need to be quick with some of our calculations. But quick doesn't mean breakneck speed. Quick means timely, not necessarily immediate.

The only mathematical experience I've ever had that required giving an immediate answer was being quizzed on the multiplication tables in elementary school. We used to play a game in fifth grade called Around the World. It was a math drill. Mrs. Schneiderman, my fifth-grade teacher, drew a large circle on the board and wrote the numbers up to 12 around it, in mixed-up order. Then she'd write another number, also 12 or less, in the middle of the circle.

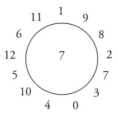

Then, with her pointer, one of those wooden ones with a rubber tip, she'd go "around the world," pointing at a number outside the circle and calling a student's name at the same time. If the number inside was 7, and she pointed at the 8 outside the circle, and she called your name, then you'd better be ready to spit out 56. Mrs. Schneiderman wouldn't point in order around the circle, even though the numbers were already mixed up. You never knew which number she would point at next or which student's name she would call.

I knew the multiplication tables cold. Even 7 times 8, which is one of the tougher ones to remember. (I don't know why 7 times 8 is hard, but it is. Ask any teacher which of the multiplication facts give kids trouble, and I bet 7 times 8 will be one of them.) But my heart pounded throughout this game. Some game! It was definitely not fun. Except for Jerome. Gads, he was good at Around the World. He never missed. He was confident. A bit smug, maybe, but I had to acknowledge his skill. He was good. I was impressed.

But the game was not even close to being fun for me. The chance of being humiliated was too great. Mrs. Schneiderman, to her credit, didn't do anything horrible to us when we were wrong. She'd just keep her pointer on the same number and call another student's name. But that was enough to make you feel bad. Around the World didn't do much for making math popular with most kids.

Fortunately for me, being impressed by Jerome didn't diminish my own feeling that I, too, was good in math. After all, I knew my facts and most often was right in Around the World.

But I know there were lots of kids who gave up on mathematics because of this kind of experience. They thought, erroneously, that knowing the times tables was the most important measure of being good in math. That's what school emphasized, so why should they have thought otherwise? Many of these children wound up as math-fearing adults.

One day in February a few years ago, Dee Uyeda, a teacher in Mill Valley, California, told her class of third graders that they were going to take a math test. The children had been studying multiplication and Dee was interested in their progress.

Jonathan's hand shot up. "Is this a timed test?" he asked.

Dee was caught by surprise. She hadn't intended to impose a time limit and had never done so before in class. Jonathan's question prompted Dee to digress a little; she asked the children about their experiences with timed tests. Their responses poured out. After hearing their reactions, Dee asked the children to put their thoughts in writing.

Jess wrote: *I don't like timed tests because the teachers never give you enough time and when I have a timed test I start to tremble with fear.*

Emily wrote: *I hate time test when I try to do them I think oh no the time is running out and I look at the paper next to me and it's half way done and I've only done one problem and after that I hate math.*

And from Elizabeth came this passionate aria: *The teacher pases out the paper. Thats when the butterflys began! Your heart is in your throt! You want to get all the math promloms rigt. But there is no time to think! There is a blur of proloms to be done. Your head gets dizzy, rushing you try to finsh. No time to check over. It will have to do. I don't think I ever got all the prolmems in a timed test rigt. You get so nervs that you can't think, your palms swet. That feeling in your stomick is too bad for words. The dreaded time test . . .*

While I was writing this book, I found I talked about little else with friends. House guests were staying with us when I was working on this chapter, and I was giving them the gist of it while we were preparing dinner one evening. Becky stopped cutting carrots and said, "I remember timed tests. I remember them

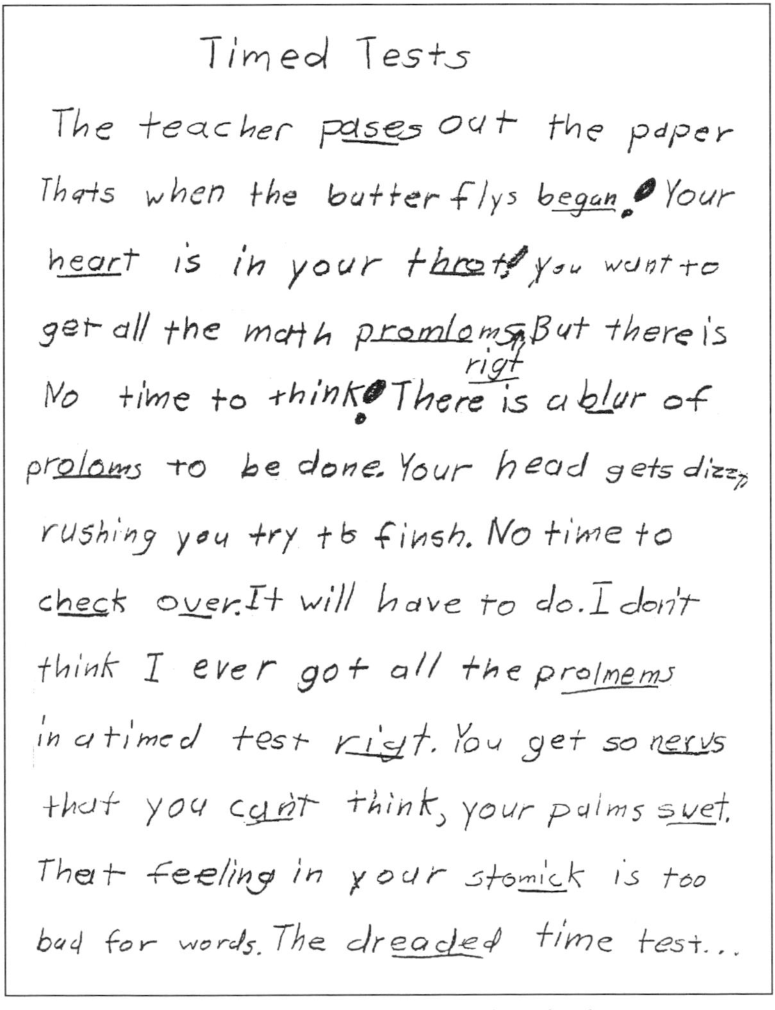

Timed Tests

The teacher pases out the paper
Thats when the butterflys began. Your
heart is in your throt! You want to
get all the math promloms. But there is
No time to think. There is a blur of
proloms to be done. Your head gets dizzy,
rushing you try to finsh. No time to
check over. It will have to do. I don't
think I ever got all the prolmems
in a timed test rigt. You get so nervs
that you cant think, your palms suet.
That feeling in your stomick is too
bad for words. The dreaded time test...

FIG. 5.1 *Elizabeth, a third grader, vividly describes her experiences with timed tests.*

in third grade. You were given a paper to do as fast as you could. When you were done, you raced up to the teacher's desk to hand it in. There was always a race to be first. I hated it."

Jeff, Becky's husband, didn't remember timed tests at all, but their son, Brian, did. Brian was just beginning fifth grade, and he remembered his second-grade experience. "You had to do a hundred problems. The teacher set a timer and when it went 'bing,' you had to hand your paper in. The teacher marked them and then read out everyone's score. You had to get 90 percent to move ahead or else you stayed on the same level and had to take the same test over again until you got 90 percent. I always tried to go over my paper to see if I was right, but I could never do them fast enough."

The next day I received an e-mail with a similar message from a friend whom I had written about my work on this chapter. (I wasn't kidding when I said that I talked about little else during this time.) She wrote a little about her own math anxiety but mostly about what had happened to her daughter: "Lisa, who does have real mathematical intuition, has been done in by timed tests. In sixth grade she had to stay in for recess when she didn't get a high enough score on these tests. In seventh grade, her math curriculum was broken into two parts: timed skills and problem solving. She was great at the problem solving—she soared, in fact. But because she flubbed these timed tests, she came away thinking she was really bad in math. She always considered these tests to be what math was really about, not the problem-solving half. It infuriated me. I couldn't reach her. And she gave up."

These are only a few stories, but they're indicative of hundreds more I've heard from people. Most of us experienced timed tests when we were in school. And the reactions expressed by the third graders, by Becky and Brian, and by Lisa's mother match those many of us have had.

The misconception about timed tests is that they help children learn the addition combinations or the times tables. This perspective makes no instructional sense. The fear of timed tests may put pressure on children to learn the facts, but I think that we can motivate children in other ways, ways that include helping them realize the benefit of knowing the facts. After all, anyone who needs to calculate mentally knows that having the facts committed to memory is a huge asset. Children can understand this.

Children who perform well under pressure display their skills well on timed tests, as my classmate Jerome did playing

Around the World. Children who have difficulty with skills or who work more slowly run the risk both of reinforcing wrong practices under pressure and of becoming fearful and negative toward their mathematics learning.

Also, the purpose of giving tests in school is to find out what children understand so that we can build from there. Timed tests don't measure what children understand but what they can recall.

The (untimed) test Dee had prepared for her class had several questions on it to help her assess what the students understood about multiplication. She knew that understanding was the bedrock on which children would be able to develop skills they could use.

One question on Dee's test was, *Show all the different ways you can prove that 6 times 7 is 42.* The children had learned how multiplication relates to addition (6 × 7 = 7 + 7 + 7 + 7 + 7 + 7), how multiplication can be shown as a rectangular array (see the illustration below), and how starting with what you know—6 times 5, for example—can help you figure out something else like 6 times 7.

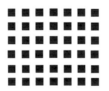

In third grade, when children typically study multiplication, they need to learn what multiplication is, how it relates to other things they've studied about mathematics, and how to apply it in a variety of problem-solving situations. Learning the times tables is important for every child, but memorization should build on, not precede, understanding. I want it all for children when they are learning mathematics—understanding and memorizing facts, in that order. I want children to learn to use numbers to solve problems, confidently analyze situations that call for the use of numerical calculations, and be able to arrive at reasonable numerical decisions they can explain and justify. Expecting any less is educationally foolish and shortsighted.

I agree that the quality of your life probably hasn't been hindered by not understanding Fermat's last theorem—or by not having even heard of it. But thinking about the price of hand lotion, the pressure of playing Around the World, and children's views of timed tests helps us understand in part why so many people were filtered out of the opportunity to learn about and understand Fermat's last theorem.

When we were in school, we weren't allowed to take our time with math problems and think about them in our own way and at our own speed. Oh, no. We had to do things fast. We had to recall addition facts instantly and recite the times tables on demand. Think? Reason? Ponder? There was no time for that in the way we were taught math. We were to get it done, get it done quickly, and get it done right. Anything else fell short.

When I got home after my meeting at the office, I took out my bottles of hand lotion. I decided that dividing the price of each container by the number of ounces in it would give me the price per ounce. I wrote down the numbers I needed to divide for each container, did the divisions on my calculator, jotted down the answers, and compared them. I did the thinking part—deciding what to do—and the calculator did the figuring part. That seemed to be an appropriate and efficient way to solve the problem.

I now had enough hand lotion to last for a year. Maybe more. Let's see, 20 ounces and 16 ounces make 36 ounces. If each day I use . . . I stopped myself.

One final note: when I got home, I checked the hand lotion I had. It was the same Vaseline Brand Intensive Care Lotion, the green container, with aloe vera. But it was a 15-ounce container. There really was a 15-ounce container! The price sticker was still on it. I had bought it at a different store, not the discount drugstore, and it had cost $4.89. Hmmm. The sale price of the 20-ounce size at the discount drugstore was $4.39. How good was this deal? Go figure.

Calculators—
Crutch or Tool?

CHAPTER 6

All of us have beliefs that we hold on to dearly, that we can't imagine abandoning, and that we're not willing to negotiate. Remember when George Bush announced that he didn't like broccoli? And remember how upset the broccoli farmers of America were? They sent him bushels of the stuff, along with heartfelt messages imploring him to give broccoli another chance. It didn't help. From what I hear, George Bush still doesn't like broccoli. No amount of persuading changed his opinion. His mind's made up.

I think our belief about whether or not children in school should be allowed to use calculators is in the same category as broccoli is for George Bush. Many people's minds are set on the idea that calculators are part of the problem in teaching math these days. And that's made me very nervous about writing this chapter.

Take the man I was talking to on the airplane, whom I wrote about in chapter 3 (the one on tip tables and percents). He believed that 85 percent to 90 percent of the people in our country are uncomfortable with math, math avoiders, or worse. He also had a strong belief about calculators. "It's terrible that they let kids use calculators in school," he said to me. "That's ruining math teaching. I don't think schools expect enough from kids."

I pursued the issue with him. "It seems to me that people

were having trouble with math even before there were calculators," I pointed out. "What worries you about children's having
calculators?"

"They don't have to think." He paused and then continued,
"They come to rely on them. They don't learn to calculate on
their own. The calculator is a crutch."

I thought for a moment about how to respond. This issue
had come up before in similar conversations, and I wanted to see
whether this man and I had some common ground on which to
talk about it.

"I've been thinking about the issue of calculators in schools
for some time, now," I said, "and I've been asking lots of people
how they use calculators. You must use a calculator as an engineer."

"I do," he replied. "I use it all the time."

"To do calculations?" I asked.

He answered, "Yes, in all sorts of ways. But, really, I use the
computer more."

"Whenever I ask people when they use a calculator or computer, I get several kinds of answers," I said. "Sometimes they use it
because it's quicker, sometimes because the numbers are too complicated to do in their head and a calculator is easier than paper
and pencil, sometimes because they want to be sure they're right."

"So you're making the argument that kids in school should
use calculators for those reasons?" he responded. "That's the
problem. They'll never learn to do the calculations themselves if
they become dependent on the calculator. What if they had to do
some calculations when they didn't have a calculator?"

"Are you ever dependent on your calculator or computer?" I
asked.

"In some cases, of course," he said. "Some of what I do is
very complicated."

"Does your computer ever go down when you need to do
some calculation or get some information?" I asked.

"Rarely," he said. "Hardly ever."

"And if it did?"

"It wouldn't be a life-and-death situation. But that's not an argument for saying that it's okay for kids not to learn to do math on their own. They need to know how to figure. Do you know what happens in a store when their computer goes down? The clerks can't even make change! They're helpless unless the machine tells them how much money to give back to a customer! It's an embarrassment. That's what I'm talking about."

"I agree," I said. "I've had that happen to me in stores, too. Let's talk about how people do figure change when they don't have a cash register that does it for them. If you bought a loaf of bread for $1.39 and gave the clerk $2.00, how would the clerk figure out the change?"

"They'd count out the change on their own," he said.

"How?"

"Oh, something like a penny makes 40 cents, a dime makes 50 cents, and two quarters makes a dollar. Let's see, that's 61 cents in change."

"You really didn't need to know it was 61 cents," I said. "It was enough to give back a penny, a dime, and two quarters."

"Yeah, I guess so," he agreed. "What's your point?"

"Were you taught that kind of shopkeeper figuring in school math?" I asked.

"I can't remember. I don't think so," he answered. "But I learned how to think, and so I can do it anyway, whether or not I was taught exactly that in school."

"When you were in school, suppose you were given the problem of figuring out how much change there would be from $2.00 after buying a loaf of bread for $1.39. How would you have done it?" I asked.

"I would have used paper and pencil," he said, "and subtracted."

"Me, too," I said. "I was taught how to subtract with borrowing, and this might have been an example of when I'd use the skill."

"So, what's your point?" he asked again.

"What I was practicing in school, spending most of my time on paper-and-pencil calculations, wasn't the skill I needed in order to be able to figure change in real life," I answered.

"So you think you didn't need to learn to subtract?" he said. "You think kids today should be able to use a calculator to do those kinds of problems?"

"I think kids today should be able to do problems like that in their head," I answered. "I think that not enough emphasis was put on thinking and reasoning when I was in school. We learned procedures and were dependent on them. We weren't taught to think and reason. I don't want kids to be dependent on a procedure or a calculator in situations when they should be able to reason for themselves. And for arithmetic problems that are complex and tedious, I want them either to be able to come up with a reasonable estimate if an estimate will suffice or to use a calculator if an accurate answer is required."

"That's nuts!" he said. "That's just the kind of thinking that's ruining our schools."

"Wait a minute," I said. "You said before that you thought 85 to 90 percent of the population don't like math, don't feel competent mathematically, and avoid math whenever they can."

"That's right," he said, "I'll stick with that. But those people learned how to do simple arithmetic."

"Yes," I said, "they probably were taught the same way I was how to add, subtract, multiply, divide, work fractions, do decimals and percents. And look how they've wound up. What was so terrific about how we were taught? It's resulted in a horrendous problem, with huge numbers of people being math phobic."

"So tell me how the calculator is going to fix that," he challenged.

I stopped to think. What he had just said gave a twist to our discussion. I thought the question was, Should children have access to calculators when learning math? What he said implied that the question now was, How would giving students access to calculators fix the problem that so many Americans do poorly with math? I wasn't arguing for calculators as a quick fix to the problem, but for a major shift in how we teach children mathematics. The critical question is, What should we be teaching in math class when every child has a calculator? Pages of paper-and-pencil computational practice are most certainly pointless with a calculator in hand. I took a deep breath and plunged in.

"The calculator isn't the answer, nor is it the problem," I said. "The calculator is a tool that should be readily available to everyone. It's a tool that children need to learn to use when appropriate, not to depend on at the expense of learning to think, reason, and solve mathematical problems."

"So you really think my second grader should be able to use a calculator to get the answers on his math homework?" he asked.

"I think the question isn't whether or not your child should be able to use his calculator on homework, but what's on the homework paper that your child is expected to do," I said.

"Don't second graders learn to add and subtract?" he asked.

"Yes," I answered. "Second grade is an important time for developing number sense and learning to add and subtract."

"So how is a calculator going to help them do that?" he wanted to know. "Don't they have to learn to think?"

"Yes," I said, "learning to think is what learning math should be all about. Classroom lessons and homework assignments should focus on challenging children to think, not on having them merely practice procedures they learned in class. They can do that without thinking. And it's no way for them to learn to like or appreciate math."

"So what kind of homework would you give so that they had practice with adding and subtracting?" he asked. "Or do you think that practicing isn't necessary in math?"

"Yes, practice is needed," I responded, "but I'd like to see the practice come in ways that also support thinking and reasoning. Maybe your second grader could be asked to figure out all the possible ways to show 20 as the sum of three numbers. Not only would he get a lot of practice figuring, but he'd also have the extra challenge of deciding how he knew when he found all of the different ways."

"That's okay for easy numbers," he said. "What about later on, when the numbers get bigger?"

"There are lots of teaching materials available today that help teach number sense and computation in ways that also support thinking and reasoning, but we're getting away from the calculator issue. If I ask children to find all the ways to represent 20 as the sum of three numbers, I don't want them to have to reach for a calculator. I want children to realize when it's easy to figure in their head and to do so. And I want them to know when it makes more sense to use a calculator, how to use it, and how to judge if the answer the calculator gives them makes sense. You don't take away pencils from children because you want them to think in their head. A pencil is a tool, and the child is in control of when to use it and what to do with it. It should be the same with the calculator."

"Look," he said, "it sounds like you're a very good teacher. You've obviously thought a lot about this. I just can't agree."

There was an uncomfortable silence. We both seemed ready to give up the conversation. I got up to use the rest room and when I returned, he was reading. We didn't speak again.

But on my way to the rest room and back, I thought of another point I wanted to make. I wanted to emphasize again that the instructional goal of mathematics is to teach children how to think, reason, and solve problems and that I didn't believe that a calculator would cause a child not to think. And even more than that, I wanted to tell him, the calculator can be a useful tool to help children think about important mathematical ideas.

I remembered a calculator activity I presented to a class of third graders. The children had been studying multiplication, and all of their work had been with whole numbers. Although it's not typical to introduce third graders to decimals, I saw the opportunity to use calculators to help the children develop a beginning sense of decimals while at the same time honing their multiplication estimation skills.

To introduce the activity, I started with what they knew—multiplication of whole numbers. I wrote on the board: $5 \times \_\_ = 30$. "What number do I need to multiply by 5 to get 30?" I asked the class. Hands shot up. This was easy. I did a few more examples like this, choosing numbers the children were familiar with.

Then I wrote on the board: *5 × __ = 85.* This required the children to estimate, and many were eager to guess.

"Rather than hearing your guesses," I said, "tell me what you know that could help you think about this."

"What do you mean?" Patrick asked.

"Well, I know that 5 times 10 is 50, so 10 is too small," I said.

"And 100 is too big," Lisa said, "because 5 times 100 is 500."

"Way too big!" Ryan added.

"Twenty is too big, too," Brian said.

"How do you know?" I asked.

"Well, if 5 times 10 is 50, then 5 times 20 is double, so it's 100," he said. Not all the children followed Brian's thinking. Being able to reason like this is difficult for many children at this age, but Brian's comment clicked with Vanessa.

"Then I guess 15," she said. "That's in between."

The children looked at me for confirmation.

"So you're guessing that 5 times 15 is 85?" I asked Vanessa. She nodded.

"How about checking it on the calculator?" I suggested, and the children eagerly reached for their calculators. Not only was the calculator a valid tool for checking their thinking, using the calculator for this example would prepare the children for what I had planned to follow.

The children quickly found that 5 times 15 was only 75. With a little experimenting, however, they proved that 17 was the missing number in the equation. When we talked about how they found the answer, all of the children reported that they experimented by pressing 5, the times key, then a number, and then the equals key. None thought to divide 85 by 5. This didn't surprise me, as the children hadn't had much experience with division and hadn't yet learned about the relationship between multiplication and division.

Next I wrote on the board: *5 × __ = 86.*

"Can we use the calculator?" Amber asked.

"Yes," I said. Most heads lowered as the children tried 5 times

18. Only three students in the class—Josh, Lisa, and Brian, the most savvy numerical thinkers—kept gazing at the equation on the board.

"This is a hard one," Josh said.

"Why do you think that?" I asked.

"Eighty-six doesn't end in a 5 or a zero. It won't work," he answered.

By this time, all of the children had discovered the difficulty. Some wailed their complaints.

"Nothing works."

"Eighteen is too big."

"You can't do it."

"Remember when we were talking about the size of the paper we write on?" I asked. "Who remembers how much it measures?" I waited until about half of the children had raised their hand and I called on Grace.

"It's $8\frac{1}{2}$ inches by 11 inches," she reported correctly.

"Yes," I confirmed. "When we measured the width of the paper, the $8\frac{1}{2}$-inch side, we first found that it was longer than 8 inches but shorter than 9 inches."

"Oh, yeah," Nick remembered. "It was in the middle, so it was $8\frac{1}{2}$."

"And remember we talked about how you could show $\frac{1}{2}$ on the calculator?" I prodded.

"It was .5," Vanessa answered.

"We tested it," Lisa added. "We added 1.5 and 1.5 and got 3, and we knew that was right because $1\frac{1}{2}$ plus $1\frac{1}{2}$ is 3."

"Oh, I get it, we need one of those in between numbers, like 17.5," Patrick said excitedly. Again, the children's heads lowered. When they found that 5 times 17.5 was 87.5, some immediately got discouraged and felt stuck while others kept trying other numbers.

Gabe was one of the students who was confused. "What are you doing?" he asked Brian.

"Trying smaller numbers," Brian said. "Look, try 17.4 or 17.3 or something."

"Oh," Gabe said, and went back to work. I've found that in

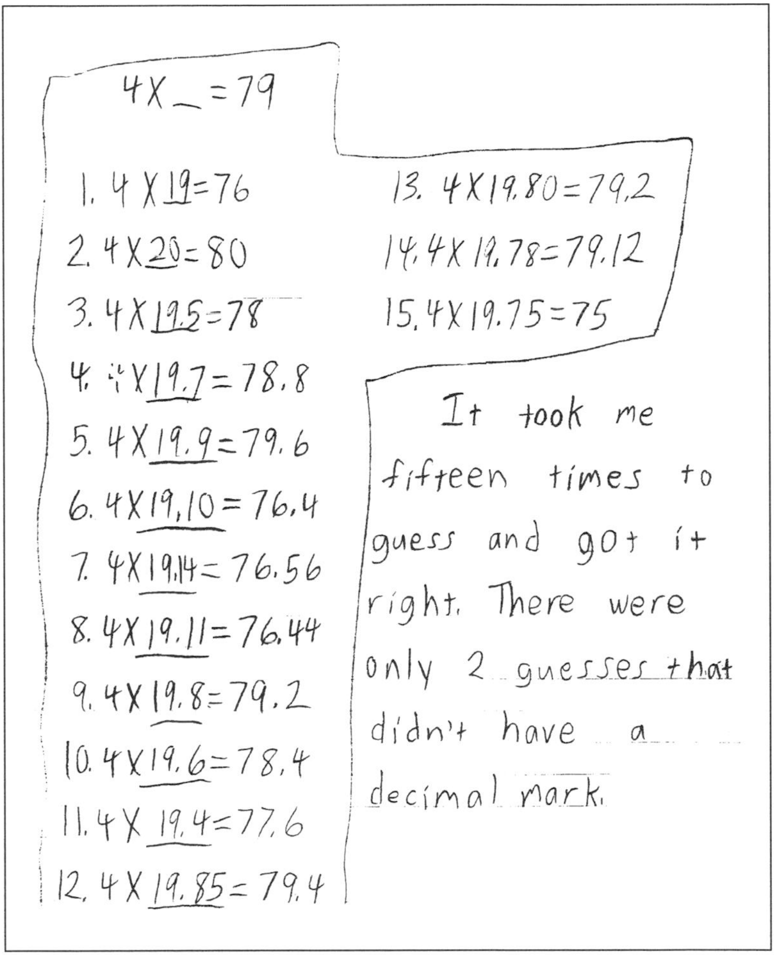

$$4X\_ = 79$$

1. $4 X \underline{19} = 76$
2. $4 X \underline{20} = 80$
3. $4 X \underline{19.5} = 78$
4. $4 X \underline{19.7} = 78.8$
5. $4 X \underline{19.9} = 79.6$
6. $4 X 19.10 = 76.4$
7. $4 X 19.14 = 76.56$
8. $4 X \underline{19.11} = 76.44$
9. $4 X \underline{19.8} = 79.2$
10. $4 X \underline{19.6} = 78.4$
11. $4 X \underline{19.4} = 77.6$
12. $4 X \underline{19.85} = 79.4$

13. $4 X \underline{19.80} = 79.2$
14. $4 X \underline{19.78} = 79.12$
15. $4 X \underline{19.75} = 75$

It took me fifteen times to guess and got it right. There were only 2 guesses that didn't have a decimal mark.

FIG. 6.1 *Patrick, a third grader, used his calculator to hone in on the answer to a multiplication problem typically reserved for older students.*

the classroom children are often helpful resources for one another.

After a minute, some children had found the correct answer of 17.2, and those who hadn't were close behind. Soon all had verified with their calculators that 5 times 17.2 was 86.

"Ready for another?" I asked. They all were. I told them that this time I wanted them each to keep a record of all the multiplications they tried in order to find the answer. "I'll give you several problems to work on," I told them, "and as you do them, see if you can get the answer in as few guesses as you can."

I wrote five problems on the board and the children dove in. (Patrick's investigation of $4 \times \underline{\hspace{1cm}} = 79$ is shown in figure 6.1.)

We did problems like these for several days, and I made them increasingly more difficult; some of the answers had two or three decimal places. The children enjoyed the challenges, and I was pleased to see their ability to estimate improve and watch them become comfortable using decimals.

William Seward Burroughs invented the first reliable adding machine in 1886. From 1905 until 1914, the Burroughs Adding Machine Company manufactured adding machines that were considered spectacular by the standards of the time. The smallest model measured 19 inches deep and was more than a foot tall. It weighed more than 60 pounds. Burroughs launched an ambitious advertising campaign with the slogan, *Don't be a calculator, buy one!* Not bad advice then, and not bad advice today.

The cost of Burroughs adding machines ranged from $300 to more than $900. Today we spend much less for pocket-size calculators that are much more powerful. Even the simplest calculators today, available for a mere $5.00, can add, subtract, multiply, divide, do percents, and take square roots—and they even have memories. They're a useful tool, practically a birthright along with pencils, paper, crayons, scissors, and books. Knowing how and when to use them is important for children to learn.

CHAPTER 7

Making Math
Make Sense

W hat's all that wrong with the way many of us were taught math? What's wrong with teaching children arithmetic procedures even if they don't understand why the procedures work? Isn't it important for children to have a firm foundation of skills that they can later apply to solving problems?

Plenty is wrong with this approach, I say. Most important, it has little to do with what we know about how children—or people of any age, for that matter—learn.

Most of us learned to play Monopoly when we were children. I remember when I learned. One day, my older sister invited me to play the game with her and her friends. I was thrilled to be playing with the older girls. I didn't know much about what to do, but they gave me a piece to move, dealt out money to me, and let me join in. They gave me advice. "Go on, buy it," they'd urge when I'd land on a property. I'd shake my head no. I didn't want to give up any of my precious money.

I didn't do very well at first. I got the part about rolling the dice and moving my piece along. I was clueless, however, about the importance of buying properties, much less building houses or hotels. I was regularly wiped out quickly, but I didn't mind. Being able to play was exciting enough for me. Over time, from more experiences with playing, I began to catch on to what the game was about, learned the importance of acquiring and developing property, and eventually became a fair enough Monopoly player.

How did this learning occur? By having the chance to play and, therefore, seeing the whole picture of the game. There were no skill drills, no separate practice rolling the dice and moving my piece, no practice merely reading Chance or Community Chest cards, no practice passing Go and collecting $200. I learned the skills from the act of playing, not in any particular sequence and not isolated from the game.

This is how we all learned to speak and understand our first language, by being in the soup of it all. From infancy on, we heard language spoken around us all the time. We tried out sounds and we learned from the responses we received. In the full complexity of all the sounds we heard and gurgled, we learned to pick out the sound patterns that make up our language and we learned the meaning of words.

A friend came to visit one day with her three-year-old daughter. She gave her daughter a book to look through and said, "How about resting on the couch while Marilyn and I talk for a little while?" Martha was hoping Maria would take a nap. Maria took the book, went across the room, and perched on a chair.

"I said sit on the couch, Sweetie," her mother said, "not on the chair." Maria got up, looked around, then sat on the couch.

"That's right," her mother said.

Martha wasn't making a conscious choice to teach Maria the difference between *couch* and *chair*. The lesson was embedded in the situation. That's the way children figure out the meaning of most words—within the context of their daily experiences. It's an incredible accomplishment, but one that occurs naturally as children process the information they receive and the experiences they have.

Children also figure out, from the full complexity of the sounds they hear, much of the structure of our grammar. When I was on recess duty at school one day, a first grader came up to me with a loud complaint.

"He hitted me," he said, pointing to a classmate.

While I was focused on resolving the social situation, I also marveled to myself at the child's grammatical structure. He had figured out that adding *ed* to a verb changed it to the past tense. How exciting! *Hitted* is incorrect, I know, but I didn't worry about that. The child would eventually hear *hit* used correctly in the past tense as well as in the present tense often enough that he would no longer make the error. None of us acquired the skill of adding *ed* to make a verb past tense from an isolated lesson that we received at home or in school. We acquired the skill from being immersed in the real purpose of using language to communicate.

We are all natural born learners and unless we have some mental handicap, all of us are curious and capable of learning many things. I agree that people have different natural talents, that some children are athletically more gifted than others, some are artistically more inclined, some possess mechanical abilities and like to take things apart and put things together. Children are not all the same. But how come mathematics has become so elusive for so many people? Before they begin school, most children are fascinated by numbers and love to count. They're eager to explore shapes and they learn the names of shapes easily. They're curious about measuring and sorting and do so whenever they have the opportunity. What happened in school mathematics that ruined the subject for so many of us?

Quite simply, anything known about how children learn was ignored once our school math learning began. We received a steady diet of textbook problems and worksheets—learning sums, then differences, then times tables—marching in a strict hierarchy up the grades. We didn't learn to consider addition and subtraction together and think of them as opposites, as two different ways to think about putting quantities together and taking them apart. We didn't see how multiplication and division related to addition and subtraction, much less to each other. While we learn naturally by being immersed in the full complexity of life, school math is taught in separate and isolated bits and pieces, and the technique hasn't worked for too many people.

I began taking piano lessons when I was seven or eight years old. I remember learning to read notes and play scales and memorizing the sharps and flats for each key. These things were basic to learning to play the piano, just as we may think of arithmetic facts and procedures as being basic to learning mathematics.

There's a big difference, however, between the way I was taught to play the piano and the way I was taught mathematics. Before learning to play the piano, I'd had many opportunities to hear music played on the piano. I'd seen people play the piano—in person and in movies. I'd watched and listened to my mother play the few songs she knew. In my very first piano lesson, I was invited to learn to play a song. Making music was part of my learning, and each new piece of music I tackled taught me new skills and gave me the chance to practice what I already had learned.

Yes, I did practice scales, arpeggios, and other exercises in isolation from playing music. But I was always clear that my goal for learning to play the piano was to play music.

Three of my aunts came to visit regularly and showed interest in what I was learning on the piano.

"I'd love to hear you play a song," Aunt Freda would say.

"What piece can you play for me?" Aunt Florrie would ask.

"Come, darling, play something on the piano," Aunt Gertie would coax.

And I would give a short performance, pleased by their interest and bathed in their attention. I continued studying the piano all through high school, which amounted to almost ten years of lessons. Never, never, in all of those years, did Aunt Freda, Aunt Florrie, or Aunt Gertie ask me to play scales or arpeggios. It was music they wanted and expected to hear.

So who cared about my ability to play scales, arpeggios, and other exercises? My piano teacher did, and she had me do so for part of my one-hour lesson each week. But the bulk of each lesson focused on the music I was learning to play, and most of the teaching of skills—helping me with fingering, playing difficult passages, interpreting the music—was done in the context of the music I was studying.

What's the parallel with math? While I never lost sight that making music was the reason for learning to play the piano, when learning math I never got even a glimpse of anything beyond learning skills. All I experienced for the first several years of school was a steady diet of pages of practice with arithmetic skills, with a little bit of measurement and learning about shapes thrown in.

I thought doing arithmetic exercises was doing math. It isn't. Doing math has to do with thinking and reasoning about problems or situations that call for applying mathematical ideas and skills. The skills are part of doing math, of course, but for a purpose, not as ends in themselves. Skills should be learned in the context of problems and situations and should not exist isolated from the problems and situations that give them their purpose.

Suppose you're teaching children how to play basketball. Imagine that for the first year, you teach them to dribble and they practice only that. The next year, you move on to passing and catching the ball. The next year is devoted exclusively to learning how to shoot baskets. Then you concentrate on the rules of the game, assigning lots of worksheet exercises, which the children complete while seated at desks, working alone and not talking to others. What a ridiculous way to learn to play basketball, and just as ridiculous a way to learn mathematics. While math isn't a team sport, it's not a spectator activity, either. An old proverb states, *I hear and I forget; I see, and I remember; I do, and I understand.* That holds true for basketball *and* mathematics.

The solution? Immerse children in doing mathematics by involving them in activities, explorations, and experiments in which they use mathematics and, by so doing, learn mathematical concepts and skills. Let children learn mathematical concepts and skills in the context of thinking, reasoning, and solving problems. I don't mean to imply that this solution is an easy one. Teaching is not a simple craft. To teach math well requires an understanding of mathematics, an appreciation of mathematics, an interest in how children learn, and the skills to be able to manage a classroom so that it invites learning.

The memory I have of my own schooling is sitting at my own desk, doing my own work on my own paper, not being allowed to talk to anyone, using my hand to shield my work from the eyes of classmates. As a teacher in a classroom, I've replaced that image with one of students actively engaged, talking in small groups, listening intently to one another, taking time alone to write about their thinking, participating in class discussions in which students present and talk about their ideas. The room is alive with mathematics!

In chapter 2, in the kitchen with Rosie, I write about Pi. At the end of the chapter, I explain that pi is the number you get when you divide the length of the circumference of any circle by the length of the circle's diameter: "For every circle, the circumference is close to 3.14 times as large as the diameter." The formula to represent this idea is sometimes written as $c = \pi d$ or $c = 2\pi r$.

I could say that I've *taught* you what pi means. But that doesn't mean that you've *learned* what pi is, that you now understand more about it. You may, but if you don't, then you need to get involved and think about this relationship. It may help if you measure the circumferences and diameters of ten or so circular objects and divide to find out how many times as long each circumference is than each diameter. Learning means to understand, not to recite back what has been said to you. Learning mathematics means to grasp relationships, see connections among ideas, and be able to use new concepts and skills in new situations.

I can also tell you that to figure out the area of a circle, you multiply the square of the radius by pi. The formula for that idea is $A = \pi r^2$. But, again, my telling doesn't help you understand how someone might have figured out that formula or why it makes sense.

Good teaching calls for helping you understand that this formula makes sense, as do all mathematical formulas, and motivating you to search for *how* it makes sense. A good teacher finds a way to help you do so.

Maybe you're wondering why you should care about the formula for finding the area of a circle. Well, I hope that you're curious, at least a little.

Several years ago, I was teaching a unit about circles to a class of seventh graders. The students measured and compared the circumferences and diameters of many circular objects, they used various methods to approximate the areas of many circles, and they had many discussions about the data they were gathering and the ideas they were thinking about.

One of the problems I gave the students was to investigate how pizzas were priced. Their assignment was to check out prices for a particular kind of pizza in each of the available sizes. They were to see whether the prices had any relationship to the areas of the circular pizza pans and determine which size was the best buy. (By "best buy" I meant the most pizza for the money.) Students collected information about sizes and prices of pizzas from several different pizza places, analyzed the information, and then compared their results.

The unit on circles was interesting to these students not only because circles were related to pizzas but because the children were actively involved, creating their understanding for themselves. They weren't told to memorize formulas and apply them to textbook examples. They were given opportunities to learn about why the formulas make sense and how they might be used.

So why does πr^2 make sense for figuring out the area of a circle? If you're interested, check problem 4 in the answer key for an explanation. But remember that merely reading what I write isn't enough. You'll have to think about my words in order to bring meaning to them for yourself.

That's the major part of learning: figuring things out in order to understand them for yourself. A teacher or a book can set you in a direction, offer some information, and explain some ideas, but you have to construct the understanding for yourself. My sister's friends encouraged me to buy properties when I was learning to play Monopoly, but I had to figure out for myself why that made sense. Maria's mother gave Maria the chance to differentiate between a couch and a chair, but it was Maria who had to sort out the information. I could have corrected the first grader's grammar and told him to say "he hit me" instead of "he hitted me," but he had to figure out that sometimes there are exceptions to patterns and that this was one of those times.

It's said that you know something best when you teach it. That's because teaching requires figuring out why something makes sense and then thinking about how to present the idea so that someone else can make sense of it, too. Making sense is the very act of learning, and the source for that understanding is inside our head.

There are some things that don't require this kind of figuring out, things that you can't figure out using logical reasoning. Customs and manners are in that category. There is no logical reason why Thanksgiving comes on a Thursday, why we set a table by putting the fork on the left of the plate and the knife and spoon on the right, or why nodding our head up and down means we are saying yes or agreeing. These are social customs that rely on convention, not on any logical structure.

Mathematics, however, relies on logical structures. On relationships. On connections between and among ideas. I had a third-grade student proudly tell me one day that she knew that 6 times 8 was 48.

"How do you know?" I asked her, curious because we hadn't yet begun to study multiplication, and also curious why she had singled out that one fact.

She recited, "Goin' fishing, got no bait, 6 times 8 is 48."

"Ah," I said, "that's right, 6 times 8 is 48. What about 6 times 6?"

"I don't know," she shrugged. "I haven't learned that one yet." And she skipped away.

She had learned the answer to 6 times 8 as part of a nonsense rhyme. She had no sense that there is some logic to why 6 times 8 is 48, that understanding multiplication has to do with understanding the logic, not memorizing facts. She was approaching multiplication as if it were a convention, not a logical concept.

Children are too often taught mathematical procedures this way. "When the sum is 18, you carry the 1 up to the next column." "When the top number is smaller than the bottom number, you have to borrow, see like this." "To do long division you divide, then multiply, then subtract, then bring down." "After the decimal point, you can drop the zeros." When we learn mathematics this way, we are following rules, not seeking to understand.

There are social conventions, however, even in learning mathematics. The symbols we use to represent ideas—numerals for quantities, π for the relationship between diameter and circumference—are social conventions. They help us communicate about mathematics. But they don't help us understand mathematics.

Think about a Coke can. You can probably show with your hands a fairly close approximation of the height of the can. You can also probably show with your hands a fairly close approximation of the diameter of the top of the can. Imagine that you take a piece of string, wrap it around the can, and cut it to that length. (The string would be the length of the circumference of the can.) Now imagine holding that string up to compare it with the height of the can. Would the string be shorter than the height of the can, taller, or about the same length?

Think about that for a moment.

Then try it.

And check problem 5 in the answer key if you're curious about the result and why it makes mathematical sense.

School Math Then, School Math Now

CHAPTER 8

About half our colleges and universities today, and many of our high schools, are using the same textbook for their beginning calculus course. Fourteen math teachers from various universities and high schools across the country produced the textbook. The group was based at Harvard and was funded by a grant from the National Science Foundation.

I recently bought a copy of this text (*Calculus*, Deborah Hughes-Hallett et al., John Wiley, 1994), and I think it's terrific. It's not that I'm having a whale of a time reading the book. Reading math texts requires more than turning pages. But for starters, a section of the preface inspired me. It tells students how to learn from the book.

"This book may be different from other math textbooks that you have used," the section begins, "so it may be helpful to know about some of the differences in advance." We're then told that this book emphasizes the meaning of the symbols used and that we should expect much less emphasis on "plug-and-chug" and using formulas and much more emphasis on interpreting formulas. We're told that the main ideas of calculus will be presented in plain English and that we'll often be asked to explain our ideas in words. We're told that there will be many open-ended problems that have more than one correct approach and more than one correct solution. It's assumed that we'll have access to a calculator or computer and we're told to use our own judgment about when to use it. (I wish I'd had this book with me when I was talking to the engineer on the airplane.) The section ends by telling us what we'll get from the book if we put in a solid effort: "a real understanding of one of the most important accomplishments of the millennium—calculus—as well as a real sense of how mathematics is used in the age of technology."

The book delivers what its authors promise. Using it requires a good deal of work: you have to go through sections carefully, grapple with the ideas presented, try the problems on your own, and, if you follow the authors' recommendation, discuss them in small groups—in general, read, question, and think hard. But that's what learning calculus or any mathematics requires. And that's what all of us should have been doing all the time we were studying math in school.

The approach of this calculus textbook reflects the overall reform in math teaching that is now occurring in our country, from kindergarten on up. Math instruction today is focusing on helping students really understand the math they're studying. It's geared toward implementing the five general goals of the National Council of Teachers of Mathematics—that students should learn to reason mathematically, become mathematical problem solvers, learn to communicate mathematically, become confident in their ability to do mathematics, and learn to value mathematics.

Think back to elementary school math. What I remember about it is that it was an orderly subject. Problems all had one right answer and one right way to reach it. There were some variations in how we worked during math class. Sometimes we listened to the teacher show us the right way to do the problem. Sometimes we'd do seat work, practicing a page of textbook or worksheet exercises. Sometimes part of the class would be sent to the board to work problems while the rest of us watched, learning little as we worried that we were next.

There were tests, too. Sometimes the teacher gave us problems orally and we had to figure answers in our head. Sometimes we were given written problems. In most instances, there was time pressure. Both on tests and during class practice, we worked by ourselves, handed in our paper, and then waited for the verdict about how we had done. There were times when the teacher used a labor-saving approach and had us exchange papers and correct each other's answers. I remember it felt bad having to mark a classmate's work as incorrect. But it felt even worse to get your own paper back with answers condemned by Xs.

Along with doing computation exercises, we solved word problems. You still had to do the arithmetic correctly; the hitch was, you had to figure out what the arithmetic problem was before you could do it. With word problems, teachers were big on having us label our answers. You could lose points if you didn't remember to label your answers, and points were points.

The emphasis in math class was on what we did, not on what we understood. I remember during my own schooling dutifully carrying in addition, borrowing for subtraction, reducing fractions, counting up decimal places, and on and on. I trusted that these procedures worked, but I didn't know why they worked. I object to having been taught to do things without also having been expected to understand what I was doing, why I was doing it, and why what I did worked.

Hey, you might be asking, what's your beef? You came out mathematically all right. You even have a college degree in math.

That's true. But I take issue with having been expected, even allowed, throughout my math learning, to learn without a simultaneous emphasis on understanding. My vendetta is against the "yours is not to question why, just invert and multiply" and other rule-bound teaching I write about in chapter 4. The result of that kind of teaching has been devastating to too many people.

I heard a joke a while ago, a used-car-salesman joke. "I sold the car," the used-car salesman tells his boss, "but the guy didn't buy it." Imagine this as a teacher joke: "I taught the math, but the kids didn't learn it." Both are unkind. The first slanders people who sell used cars. The second not only slanders teachers but also pinpoints the hurt many of us experienced as victims of that kind of teaching.

Maybe you're thinking I'm a bit too touchy about all this, that I shouldn't expect everyone to understand everything in the world. We can all drive a car without understanding how the engine works. We can bake a cake without understanding the chemistry that causes it to rise. We can use our computer, modem, and fax without understanding electronics. What's my problem?

Well, I agree that we can't expect everyone to understand everything in the world. But we're talking mathematics here, and it's very, very important for children to understand mathematics. There's a reason mathematics is one of the time-honored three Rs. If children don't understand mathematics in the early grades, they won't stick with it later on in school. Right now, once math becomes an elective in high school, 50 percent of the students elect not to take it. And unless they've continued their math studies, children today are eliminated from many career choices. Calculus is a requirement for many college majors.

Consider how math is essential in business, whether in making market predictions, preparing budgets, or coming up with estimates for a construction project. Consider how math is essential in any of the sciences or engineering. Consider medical careers, sales positions, technical jobs. Come on. It's a serious choice to check out of studying math.

I agree that we're not all mathematically gifted and not all capable or destined to spend nine years on one math problem the way Andrew Wiles did to prove Fermat's last theorem. (Check out chapter 5 if you haven't read about this yet.) I agree that some of us learn mathematics more easily than others. But most of us are perfectly capable of learning mathematics with understanding and with pleasure. It all depends on how we're taught. Everyone I talk with who remembers math class as a good experience remembers a special teacher, one who cared, took an interest, and taught in a way that made the subject accessible and that made success possible.

The current reform in math teaching is an ambitious, widespread, and courageous movement to make mathematics accessible to all students. For too long, math has been a filter that has separated students into haves and have-nots. The aim of math teaching today is for students to be either haves or have-mores.

Math classes today are different from those we experienced, both in what we're teaching and how we're teaching it. The bottom line for math lessons now is this: if students are able to be successful in math class without understanding what they're studying but merely by repeating what they were taught by rote, then the teaching simply isn't good enough. And to learn with understanding, students' curiosity about mathematics must be tapped, their thinking must be stimulated, and they have to be actively engaged in learning and doing mathematics. It's not okay to do anything less than that and call it education.

The key to math-teaching reform is to help children learn to think, reason, and solve problems. That's the kind of education that will prepare children for their future. Thinking, reasoning, and solving problems are the skills that employers are looking for in new employees. And helping children develop those skills is the way we'll keep them interested in continuing to learn mathematics.

What might today's math classes look like? It's not simple to describe the complexity of any classroom, and it's hard to offer one description that would be accurate for all classrooms. However, in the next several chapters, I present examples of math teaching that show how the spirit of the current reform efforts can be implemented to offer children the chance not only to learn important mathematics but to learn how to learn mathematics. I've chosen three grade levels to offer a range in the descriptions—second grade, fifth grade, and eighth grade. For each, I try to give you a sense of what actually occurred and, at the same time, a glimpse of the rationale behind my teaching choices.

Read on.

Teaching Addition and Subtraction

Remember second grade? In second grade, we spent most of our math time learning addition and subtraction. We learned to carry and borrow and did a great deal of paper-and-pencil practice. Also, we memorized the basic addition and subtraction facts. If we got to multiplication, it was in a limited and beginning way. Multiplication gets full attention in third grade.

I taught math to second graders for several years. Addition and subtraction are still big topics for the children, but in a different way. Worksheet drill and practice are no longer the mainstays of their learning. That's because a diet consisting mainly of practicing paper-and-pencil computation doesn't support the broader learning that children need. (Check back to page 13 in chapter 1 if you need a reminder about the current broader definition of basics.) Along with developing skill with addition and subtraction, math instruction must also develop children's number sense and build their intuition about numbers so that they become confident in their thinking and flexible in their approaches. And math teaching must stimulate children's intellectual curiosity and help them stay interested in learning mathematics.

What can happen in the classroom to accomplish this? Second graders need a great deal of experience with counting, combining, and comparing quantities so that they can begin to understand our place value system. Understanding how we group by 10s is essential for them to understand how to compute with larger numbers. Here's a sample lesson.

"How many stars do you think I can draw on the board in one minute?" I asked my second-grade class one morning. Some children ventured guesses.

"Twenty."

"Maybe a hundred."

"Lots."

At this age, children are just beginning to sort out quantities, and a large range of estimates is typical.

I then had the students use the class clock to time one minute. (Learning to tell time is also important in second grade, and we use every opportunity possible to work on this.) While the children watched the clock, I drew stars on the board as fast as I could. Finally they called, "Time!" and I stopped drawing.

"I think I drew a lot of stars," I told the children, shaking my arm to relax it. Children again guessed how many I had drawn.

"It looks like fifty."

"I think a hundred."

"I think a million."

"How can we find out how many stars I drew?" I asked.

"Count them!" they replied. Second graders love to count and they rely on counting as their major strategy for dealing with numerical situations. They count when they want to know how many there are, they count when they have to add two or more quantities, they count when they take quantities away. An important goal in second-grade math is to help children move beyond counting as their major strategy for dealing with numbers and become comfortable with other ways to add and subtract. I'll show how that can happen in a bit.

In this lesson, however, counting was appropriate. To help the children see that there are different ways to count and to give them practice doing so, I had them count the stars by 1s, 2s, 5s, and 10s. First we counted by 1s and checked off the stars as we did so. Then we circled stars in groups of two and counted by 2s. Then we circled groups of 5 and 10 to count those ways. Counting by 10 is especially important for helping children understand how our place value system works.

It isn't always obvious to children that when you count the same objects in different ways—by 1s, 2s, 5s, or 10s—you'll arrive at the same number each time. So for some of the children, this came as a surprising discovery!

After we counted the stars in several ways and verified that I had drawn 58, I told the children that now I would time one minute while they drew stars. Some children already knew how to draw the conventional five-pointed star, but others used their own version. After a short time, however, all of the children were able to draw five-pointed stars, and those who had just learned were extremely proud of their skill. I mention this as a reminder that children don't compartmentalize learning as we do. Sure it's a math lesson, but stars are part of it, and learning to draw stars while learning to estimate and count blend together for children in a seamless way.

When one minute was up, the children each counted how many stars they had drawn. I asked them to count them in different ways to be sure they were correct. As they counted, I went around the room and gave each child a sticky note on which to record the number of stars he or she had drawn. Then we organized the notes into a class graph. Learning to organize data, represent these data graphically, and interpret the information are also important to children's math learning.

I extended this one-day lesson on future days by having the children work in pairs. One child kept time for a minute while the other drew stars, dollar signs, or letters of the alphabet. Together they estimated how many items were drawn and then counted them in several ways. The children took turns, so that each of them could practice timing one minute and have the chance to draw. To the children, this activity was as much play as work. Learning should be like play, not in the sense that its goal should only be to have fun, but because it's engaging in the way play is, involving children completely with the task at hand. If learning is enjoyable, then so much the better.

Introducing a whole-class lesson that sets the stage for independent work, as in this example, is a way to manage instruction in the classroom. The teacher prepares all the students for what they're to do and then allows them to work on their own at their own pace while the teacher offers individual help as needed. This particular activity was one of several counting activities the students could do by themselves. Learning to make choices and manage time is a valuable aspect of children's learning. When it was time for independent work, they chose which activity they wanted to do, either trying a new one or returning to one they particularly enjoyed. Children enjoy doing things they like over and over, and the practice is valuable for them.

In one of the other independent counting activities—this one done individually, not with a partner—the children used popcorn kernels, lentils, and a small hollow plastic cube each side of which measured about ¾ inch. First, they estimated and then counted how many popcorn kernels would fill the cube. They recorded their estimate, then their count (which they had to do in at least two different ways), and calculated the difference. Then they had to repeat the procedure with the lentils, using the information they had discovered about popcorn kernels to estimate how many lentils would fill the cube.

A popcorn kernel is more than twice the size of a lentil. In a class discussion after all of the children had done this activity (children learn from one another as well as from the teacher), we talked about how they used this size comparison in making their estimates. Children who didn't use the information that popcorn kernels were more than twice as large when estimating the number of lentils had the chance to hear ideas from others and learn something about proportional reasoning.

I then added navy beans and split peas for them first to estimate how many would fill the cube and then to count how many did. This gave them more experience comparing sizes and using that information for their estimates.

On days when the children chose from several activities, the classroom was an active and busy place. The children were involved, some working alone and some in pairs. I was busy circulating—prodding, keeping children on track, talking with them about what they were recording or how they were counting, helping those who were having difficulty, noticing how children were thinking about the mathematics they were doing.

One day, Catherine asked for help. She had estimated the plastic cube would hold 23 popcorn kernels, had counted 29 kernels in the cube when she filled it up, and had recorded that she had counted 6 more than she had estimated. She had then estimated that 49 lentils would fill the cube, a reasonable estimate based on the comparative size of lentils and popcorn kernels. After she had filled the cube with lentils, Catherine first counted 49 of them into a pile, then counted the ones remaining into a new pile. There were 17. (See figure 9.1.) Now she was stuck. She didn't know how many 49 and 17 were altogether and she didn't want to "mess up" her piles.

It was near the end of math class, so I said to Catherine, "Why don't we ask the others for help with this? We can do that tomorrow." Catherine agreed. Her lentils were on a sheet of paper, and I carefully carried the paper to a bookshelf for safekeeping.

The next day, I explained Catherine's problem to the others. I showed Catherine's paper with the lentils and Catherine explained how she had counted them into two piles. I wrote on the board:

Catherine guessed 49 lentils.

There were 17 more.

How many lentils filled the cube?

One reason I wrote complete sentences, not just the numbers, was to keep the context in mind and not isolate the numbers from the real problem. A second reason was to model for the children how to write complete sentences and to give them some reading practice. Reading is part of math too.

I asked for ideas. Eli waved his hand.

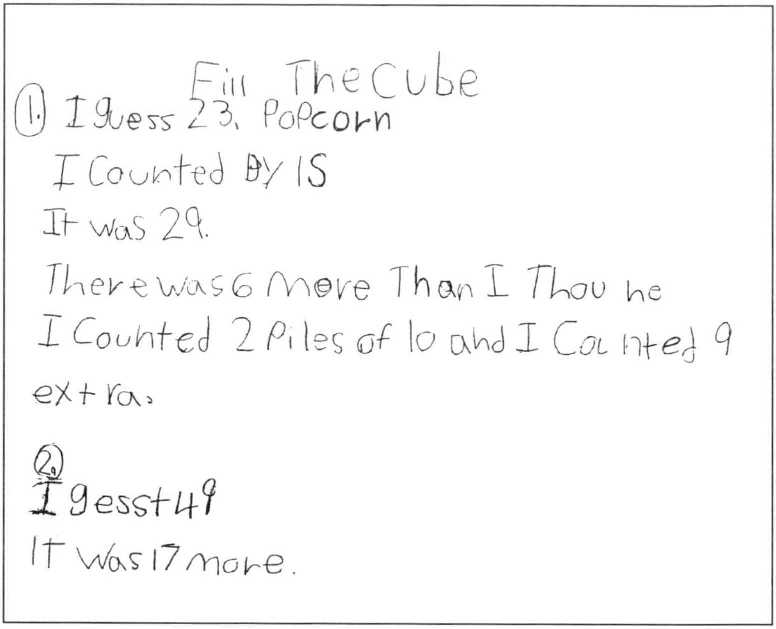

Fill The Cube
(1.) I guess 23. Popcorn
I counted By 15
It was 29.
There was 6 more Than I Thou he
I counted 2 Piles of 10 and I counted 9
extra.

(2.)
I gess+49
It was 17 more.

FIG. 9.1 *Catherine, a second grader, estimated and counted how many popcorn kernels filled a cube. After finding that it took more lentils to fill the cube than she had estimated, she was stuck about how to determine a total.*

"Just shove them together and count," he said, with a tone of impatience.

"That's one way to solve the problem," I said, "and we can do that later to check. But I'm interested in how you might figure it out in your head. Take a minute and think about how you would do this." I hadn't taught the children how to add with carrying. This was early in the year and I was more interested in pushing them to reason numerically than in teaching them one particular method of adding. I was also extremely interested in hearing the approaches they would take so I could build on their thinking and help them expand their strategies for reasoning.

A few children reached for paper and pencil. "Let's not use

paper and pencil but just talk about how you would do this in your head," I said. "You'll get a chance to write about your ideas in just a minute."

The children had a variety of approaches.

"You can count them up," Kelly said, showing how she would start at 50 and count on 17 more. She lost track on her fingers, however, and had to get a friend to help keep track. With the second try, she got to 66.

"Does anyone have a different way?" I then asked, my standard question after a student offers an idea.

Molly had a different approach. Her explanation was complicated. "You take one from the little pile and put it on the big pile and then you have 50 in the big pile and 16 in the other pile. Then you take 10 from the little pile and move them over, so now you have 60. Then you have six more and that's 66."

Rudy's approach was a combination of what Molly had suggested and what Kelly had done. "I'd take 10 from the 17 extras," he said, "and add it on to the 49 and you get 59. Then you just have seven more, so you go 60, 61, 62, 63, 64, 65, 66." Rudy used his fingers to be sure he counted on seven more.

Leslie said, "I'd get Snap cubes and count out the two piles and then snap them together and count them by 10s." (Snap cubes—interlocking cubes—are standard equipment in many elementary classrooms.)

I called on Eli again. "I'd still push them all together and count them up," he said.

After all of the children who wanted to had offered their ideas, I asked them to show how they would solve the problem with pencil and paper. I gave my standard direction, "Use numbers, words, and if you like, pictures. Make sure I can understand how you reasoned."

The children's papers (figures 9.2–9.4) showed the different ways they thought. Some recorded the approach they had described to the class; some used a method that someone else had explained. Both were fine. The class rule is that what children write has to be something that makes sense to them. "What's

Fɪɢ. 9.2 *Daniel wrote out the numbers from 49 to 66 and then counted to see how many lentils there were in all.*

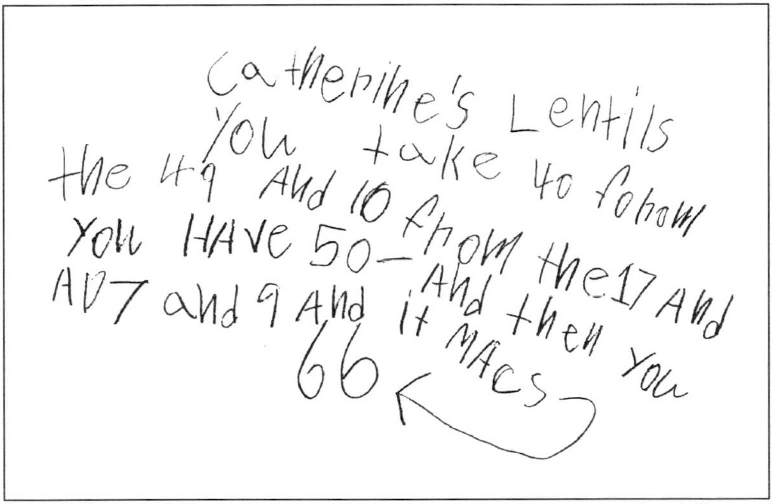

FIG. 9.3 *To add 49 and 17, David added first the tens—40 + 10— and then added on the rest.*

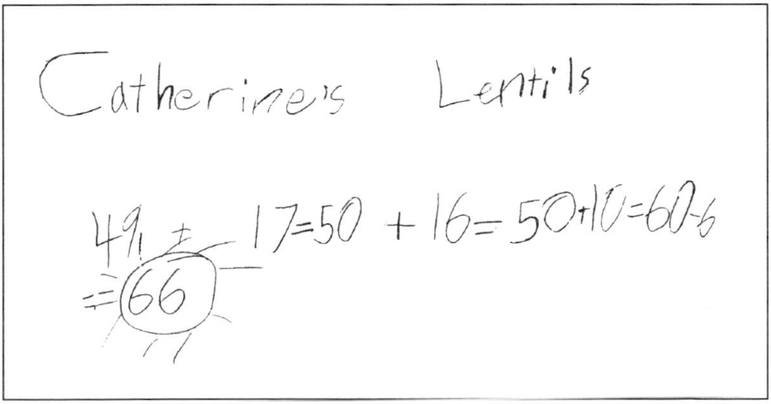

FIG. 9.4 *Ali reasoned similarly to the way David did, but expressed her thinking numerically, without words.*

most important," I tell them, "is that you understand what you do and can explain your reasoning."

The goal in teaching second-grade addition is that children should learn several strategies for adding numbers and be able to choose a method that makes sense in a particular situation. When facing an addition problem with simple numbers—20 + 25, for example—I expect the children to do it in their head. (Figuring mentally is an ongoing activity throughout the year.) When an addition problem is more complicated, like the 49 + 17 problem with the lentils, I think it's appropriate for them to use paper and pencil. For problems involving even more demanding numbers that call for tedious computations, a calculator may be an appropriate choice.

Calculators in second grade? Let's talk about this. This is a hot issue, one about which people fervently hold different views. (If you haven't read it yet, you may want to check out chapter 6.)

When I teach second graders, I make calculators as available to the children as pencils, paper, crayons, scissors, and books. This does not mean that children become dependent on calculators and won't do any math without them. Quite the opposite. Many children aren't interested in the calculators, and I have to request that they use them when I think it's appropriate that they learn how. Other children, however, are fascinated by them, figure out how to use them (including the memory keys), discover decimal numbers and demand to know what they are, and endlessly explore doing different calculations.

But even though calculators are available in the classroom, there are times when I ask the children not to use them, just as I ask them not to use paper and pencil when I want them to figure in their head. In these cases, I communicate my reasons to the children so that they understand why I am making the request.

Later in the year, we were studying subtraction. Again, think back to your own learning. I remember learning that subtraction was "take away," that you showed subtraction with a minus sign, and that sometimes you had to "borrow." And, of course, we had lots of practice subtracting, and then we did subtraction word problems.

As a teacher, I've noticed that children have difficulty with subtraction, both doing subtraction calculations and knowing when to use subtraction. The "take away" situations are usually clear to children, but there are other common situations involving subtraction. When you compare two quantities to find out how much more one is than the other, you subtract. For example, you have 35 cents and I have 17 cents. How much more money do you have? Sometimes you have to subtract in a how-many-more situation that isn't a comparison. For example, you need 12 birthday candles for the cake but you only have 7. Sometimes you're trying to figure out how long ago something happened. For example, a book was written in 1973. How many years ago was that? Sometimes you have to make change. For example, you buy a bag of potato chips for $1.79 and give the clerk $5.00.

It's obvious to most adults that these are all subtraction problems. That is, you could solve any of them by performing subtraction, either in your head, with paper and pencil, or on a calculator. But for children just learning about subtraction, the different language patterns can be confusing. It's only after experiencing many different situations that children learn to recognize which ones call for subtraction and which ones call for addition, division, or multiplication. That's why working primarily with numerical examples, not with the situations in which the numbers occur, isn't a broad enough approach.

These second graders had been involved with all kinds of subtraction problems that spring. The entire school had also been studying about oceans, and classrooms were filled with children's displays about different aspects of ocean life.

"Let's do ocean math problems," Kenny suggested one morning.

"What would they be?" I asked.

"We could do subtraction stories," Sally said.

The others were interested, and I structured an assignment

for them. I told them they each should write and solve a subtraction story problem related to oceans. I'd read the problems, talk with them about their work, and then we'd illustrate them. Open house was coming up soon, and their problems could be on display.

This went fine. At the end of the day, I had an ocean math problem from each child. When I read the problems, I realized that some of the children had used very large numbers and had used a calculator to figure the answer. For example, Doug wrote: *There were 7,444,449 fish and 256 got eaten? How many are left?* His answer was correct. I knew that Doug hadn't yet learned to read a number as large as 7,444,449. Nor could he do the calculation in his head or with paper and pencil. The calculator had allowed him to play with numbers that were out of his reach and out of the reach of most second graders.

Doug wasn't the only child who wrote a problem with tricky numbers. Marissa had written: *There were 90 purple starfish in one part of the ocean and 18 red starfish in the other part of the ocean. How many more purple starfish were there than red starfish?* As any teacher can tell you, subtracting from a number that ends in a zero is difficult for children to understand. Marissa's answer was correct, and again, the calculator had helped her.

I didn't want to discourage the children's resourcefulness, but I also wanted to make sure they understood what they were doing with the numbers. The next day, I returned the papers to the children and told them how they were to prepare their final work for the open house display. I held up paper that had the top half blank for drawing a picture and the bottom half lined for writing. (This is standard paper for young children that allows them to write and illustrate their ideas.)

"Write your subtraction problem on a sheet of paper like this," I said. "Then, on a separate sheet of paper, write your solution. I'll put all of your solutions into a booklet. That way your families can read your stories, try to figure out the answers for themselves, and then check in the booklet to see if they're right." The children liked this idea.

I gave them another direction: "When you solve the problem, please do so in two different ways. You may use the calculator for one of those ways, but you should explain how you would figure this out without the calculator, also."

For most of the children this was fine. Doug, however, blanched, as did a few others.

I gave one last direction: "If you would like to make any changes to your problem, either with the story or with the numbers, that's fine. Just raise your hand so I can talk with you about what you plan to change."

Some children, Doug included, did make changes. My conversations with them helped me assess what they understood, which is important to know when making teaching decisions. Others didn't make changes to their work. Marissa, for example, stuck with her numbers. She was able to do the subtraction, not in the traditional way that you or I were taught, but in a way that made sense to her and that demonstrated to me her numerical understanding and ability (Marissa's solution is shown in figure 9.5, on the next page).

Some additional comments about the second-grade examples I've given here. In two of the classroom examples I described, the learning experiences were initiated by the children: Catherine brought up her lentil problem, and Kenny and Sally suggested the ocean stories. I chose these examples purposely to illustrate that classroom learning should involve the children in every way possible. I don't follow up every suggestion the children make. Yikes, we'd have a cupcake party every day. But I do follow their suggestions whenever they fit my educational goals and seem appropriate. Most of what I do comes from the instructional materials I have available to me, a hefty collection from years of teaching.

Also, Catherine eventually figured out for herself that she had 66 lentils all together. She drew 17 tally marks and counted, as Kelly had demonstrated earlier. I realize that using tally marks is not an efficient way to add and not the strategy that Catherine

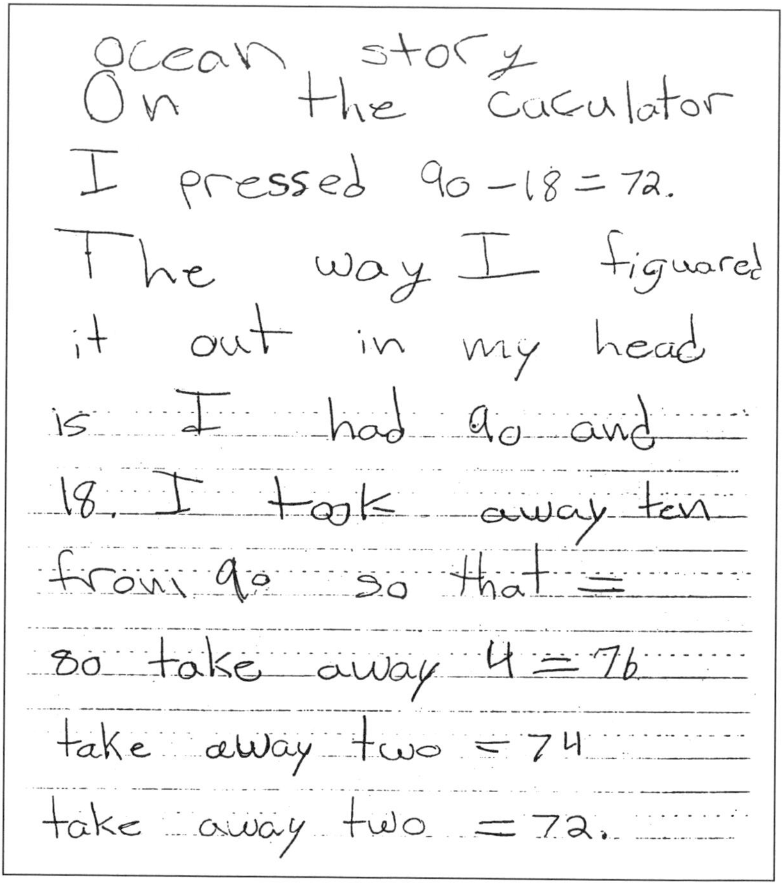

ocean story

On the cuculator

I pressed 90 - 18 = 72.

The way I figuared
it out in my head
is I had 90 and
18. I took away ten
from 90 so that =
80 take away 4 = 76
take away two = 74
take away two = 72.

FIG. 9.5   *Marissa's unique way of making sense of subtraction shows how she made sense of the problem.*

should always rely on for problems like this one. However, what Catherine did made sense to her at this time while her own math understanding and skills were emerging. By the end of the year, after more time, more experiences, and lots of encouragement and help from me, Catherine was able to give up this counting-on strategy and make numerical calculations effectively both in her head and with paper and pencil.

It's also important to note that the children's math learning during the year extended beyond learning about numbers. It included learning about geometric shapes, doing measurements of all kinds, examining statistical data, exploring patterns, and learning about probability. And in all of these areas, children were expected to think, reason, and solve problems.

And a final comment about addition and subtraction. I never demanded that children use carrying or borrowing, as most of us were taught. I never told them that there was one "best" or "right" method to use, or that there was a particular method I expected them to use. Rather, I kept the emphasis on their choosing methods that were appropriate to situations and that made sense to them.

This teaching approach meant that the children's homework assignments didn't resemble the papers I was used to taking home. More often, their homework involved extending an activity from class, such as doing Stars in One Minute with a family member and bringing in the data to add to our class graph, teaching a family member a math game they had learned, finding something at home that cost 25 cents and either bringing it in or drawing a picture of it, seeing how many people in the phone book had the same last name as theirs, or timing how long it took them to brush their teeth or get dressed in the morning. Math was lively, engaging, and related to real life.

Teaching Fractions

A major math topic in fifth grade is fractions. Remember reducing fractions? Finding common denominators? Changing improper fractions to mixed numbers? Fifth grade was the year most of us spent a good deal of time learning the ins and outs of fractions. For some of us, learning about fractions was easy, even fun. For others, it was horrible. But, easy or not, learning about fractions was mostly learning the rules for working with fractions. Too often, however, we applied the rules without thinking about the sense of what we were doing.

Here's a common error that all teachers see: when students add fractions, they add the numerators and also add the denominators. For example, students will write $\frac{1}{2} + \frac{1}{3} = \frac{2}{5}$. Students make this error for different reasons. They may have forgotten that they need to change the fractions so they have the same denominator. They may have confused the rule for adding fractions with the rule for multiplying fractions. They may just have been careless.

Whatever the reason for the wrong answer, the error indicates that making sense of the problem wasn't foremost in children's minds. It's ridiculous for children to start with $\frac{1}{2}$, add to it, and wind up with an answer—$\frac{2}{5}$—that's less than the $\frac{1}{2}$ they started with. Most students don't notice this absurdity, or even think about looking for it.

Here's an item from the National Assessment for Educational Progress test that was given in 1982:

Estimate the answer to $\frac{12}{13} + \frac{7}{8}$
a. 1
b. 2
c. 19
d. 21

Remember these kinds of multiple-choice questions? This one was on the test given to thirteen-year-olds and also on the test given to seventeen-year-olds. Only one of the choices is a reasonable contender. Since $\frac{12}{13}$ is almost 1 and $\frac{7}{8}$ is also close to 1, adding them would produce a sum pretty close to 2. So the only possible answer that makes sense is b.

What percentage of the thirteen-year-olds, the eighth graders, do you think answered the question correctly? And what percentage of the seventeen-year-olds, about to leave high school, do you think did?

The results were dismal. Among the thirteen-year-olds tested, 24 percent chose the correct answer (responses were split almost equally among the four choices); 37 percent of the seventeen-year-olds answered correctly.

I include this information about older students in a chapter about fifth grade for two reasons. The results of this test were a key factor in instigating a national push to look at how we were teaching mathematics, identify the problems, and make needed changes. And the minimally improved performance by the seventeen-year-olds on this particular question makes the case that teaching fractions to fifth graders should build understanding and focus on thinking and reasoning, not on memorizing and applying rules, so that older students will respond more sensibly.

Why have fractions always been so hard for so many students? Fractions are complicated because we use them for many different purposes in many different situations. Sometimes, for example, we use fractions to think of parts of a whole, a concept many of us learned by cutting pies into different-size pieces. Sometimes fractions represent parts of a collection of like items: you buy half a dozen cookies, or an airline sets aside a fourth of an airplane's seats for economy fares. We think of fractions as numbers and compare them as we do other numbers, thinking about $5/8$ as smaller than $7/8$, $1/3$ as larger than $1/4$, and so on. We use fractions when we measure. Rulers, for example, show halves, fourths, eighths, and sixteenths of inches, marking them as we do numbers on a number line. Fractions are related to division. For example, we change the fraction $9/2$ to $4\frac{1}{2}$ by dividing 9 by 2. (It's as if the little dots in the division symbol ÷ are each replaced by a number.) Sometimes fractions represent ratios; for example, when we say that 4 out of 5 dentists recommend something, we mean that $4/5$ of dentists do. Also, we use fractions when we think about measuring chance. When we toss a coin, for example, the probability is $1/2$ that it will come up heads; there is a $1/6$ chance of turning up a 4, or any other particular number, when rolling a single die.

Add to this wide range of uses the fact that when children do not have a firm understanding about fractions, they get easily confused. Think about children learning to compare fourths and eighths, for example. They are used to thinking that 8 is more than 4, but have to switch their thinking in order to understand that fourths are bigger than eighths. And while it isn't too complicated to help children think about why $1/8$ is less than $1/4$ (here's where thinking about pies can help), it gets more difficult when they're comparing $3/8$ and $1/3$. (See chapter 4 for a discussion of these particular fractions.)

Why were fractions invented, anyway? I don't remember this being explained to me in elementary school as information that would help me understand why I was learning about them. Fractions merely existed, and I had to learn to work with them.

Fractions were invented for a simple reason—we needed them. Pure supply and demand. We had plenty of numbers to use for counting—1, 2, 3, 4, and so on—and these numbers served us just fine for adding, subtracting, and multiplying. (Well, there was a bit of a snag if you had to subtract a larger number from a smaller one, taking 9 from 5, for example, but fractions wouldn't have helped us there. For those kinds of subtraction problems, we needed to invent negative numbers. But let's not get started on that right now.) It was division that did it. Dividing 9 into two groups, a calculation I mentioned before, puts 4 in each group with 1 left over. If you are dividing 9 apples, you can divvy up the remaining apple as well, so there are $4\frac{1}{2}$ apples in each group. We needed some way to represent this half of an apple. Fractions were an invention of necessity.

And now that we had fractions, we began to use them. We figured out how to work with fractions just as we worked with whole numbers. This, again, was out of necessity.

Children come to school already knowing some things about fractions. They've heard fractions used and have a sense about fractional parts.

"You need to eat at least half of the peas before you leave the table."

"I'll be back in around three-quarters of an hour."

"We need half a yard of ribbon for the trim."

"My, you're thirty-five and a half inches tall now."

"The dishwasher is only half full."

But young children haven't yet learned about the formal symbolism we use to represent fractions, such as $\frac{1}{2}$, $\frac{3}{4}$, or $35\frac{1}{2}$.

It makes sense that children learn fractions by building on what they already know. So it makes sense in the classroom to provide children with concrete ways to think and learn about fractions. The concrete ways can include physical materials students actually get their hands on or real-life references they can relate to. For sure, there's no single concrete material or real-life reference that will do it. We have to surround students with many ways to look at and consider fractions and give students common experiences with fractions so that class discussions can add to each individual's learning.

What might beginning fraction instruction look like in a

fifth-grade classroom? Here are some snapshots of fraction instruction I've provided to fifth graders to build on their prior knowledge and help them deepen, extend, and cement their understanding about fractions.

To introduce one of my fifth-grade classes to fractions, I talked with students about fractions that were close to $\frac{1}{2}$, the fraction all of them understood. I gave them situations and asked them to decide whether "more than one-half" or "fewer/less than one-half" was a reasonable estimate. For example, Ellen made 7 baskets out of 11 free throws. Did she make more than half or fewer than half of the shots? Or, Billy blocked 3 field goals out of 8 attempts. Were more than half or fewer than half of his attempts successful? Students then wrote their own examples and presented them to the class.

Leslie's example caused a class discussion. She had written, "I had 25 raffle tickets to sell and I sold 13 of them."

Mark said Leslie had sold more than half of her tickets.

Erin, always precise, objected. "But what if I sold 12," she said. "Then you'd say I sold less than half, and that would sound like a lot less than what Leslie sold and it was only one different."

"What do you suggest?" I asked Erin.

"I think we should be able to say 'about half' if it's really close," she said.

"Fine," I said. We added the category and took another look at the examples we had already considered.

The next day, I had each child make a fraction kit, giving directions to the entire class at once. Before the lesson, I had taken sheets of five colors of 12-by-18-inch construction paper and cut them into 3-by-18-inch strips. At the start of the lesson, I gave each child five strips, one of each color. We kept the red strip intact, folded and cut the blue strip into halves and labeled each piece, folded and cut the yellow strip into fourths, the orange strip into eighths, and the green strip into sixteenths, again labeling all pieces. (See the diagram on the next page.)

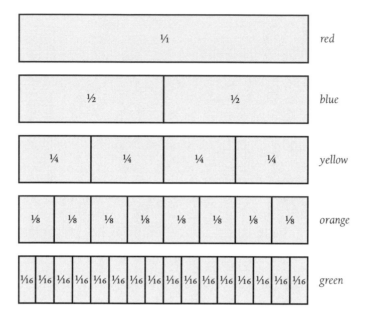

"Boy, there are a lot of those little sixteenths," Rodney said, shaking his hand to relax it after labeling his pieces. This is the kind of experience that will keep Rodney from being confused about whether $\frac{1}{2}$ or $\frac{1}{16}$ is larger.

I taught the students two games to play. For Cover Up, I made dice from wooden cubes on which I had written $\frac{1}{2}$, $\frac{1}{4}$, $\frac{1}{8}$, $\frac{1}{8}$, $\frac{1}{16}$, $\frac{1}{16}$, one number on each of the six sides. Children took turns rolling a cube and putting onto their whole red strip the piece that matched the fraction that came up. The goal was to cover the red strip entirely and to do so exactly. If a child had only a $\frac{1}{8}$ space left, for example, and rolled $\frac{1}{4}$ or $\frac{1}{2}$, she lost her turn. After playing this game, children knew that $\frac{1}{16}$ was smaller than $\frac{1}{8}$, $\frac{1}{4}$, and $\frac{1}{2}$. They understood that $\frac{3}{8}$ was less than $\frac{1}{2}$, and they could visualize and explain why this was so. They knew that $\frac{1}{2}$ and $\frac{1}{8}$ made $\frac{5}{8}$ and that they then needed $\frac{3}{8}$ more to make a whole.

When they tired of playing Cover Up, I taught them how to play Uncover. For this game, they began with their two blue halves on the red strip and tried to be the first to uncover the red strip entirely through a process of swapping equivalent pieces and removing pieces. Again, children took turns rolling a cube. They had three options on each turn—to remove a piece that was the size of the fraction face up on the cube, to exchange one of the pieces left on the red strip for equivalent pieces (to include at least one piece the size of the fraction face up on the cube), or to do nothing and pass the cube to the next player. (A player couldn't remove a piece and trade on the same turn, only one or the other.) I told the children to be sure to check one another's trades.

The comments children made while playing this game were uplifting to overhear.

Sarah's first roll was $\frac{1}{8}$. "Okay," she said, "I can exchange one $\frac{1}{2}$ for four of the $\frac{1}{8}$s."

Elissa interrupted her as she reached for the pieces. "Look," Elissa said, "just trade for one $\frac{1}{4}$, one $\frac{1}{8}$, and two $\frac{1}{16}$s. That way you'll be sure to get to take something off on your next roll."

Sarah hesitated and looked over her pieces. All of a sudden, her face lit up. "Oooh," she said, "that's neat." She did what Elissa suggested, saying as she moved the pieces, "One-half is the same as $\frac{1}{4}$ plus $\frac{1}{8}$ plus $\frac{2}{16}$."

These fraction-kit games were terrific preparation for helping students learn how to add and subtract halves, fourths, eighths, and sixteenths when fractions had unlike denominators. And they didn't need to learn a rule to do so. The concrete material gave them a way to reason with fractions. The students referred to the kit often.

In another lesson, I had the children do a good deal of thinking about sharing cookies, using paper circles to represent the cookies. To begin, I asked them to figure out how much each person's share would be if they divided one cookie among four people, then two cookies among four people, then three, four, five, and six cookies. Working in pairs, the children cut apart the paper "cookies," labeling the parts, and recording how much each person got.

When dividing six cookies among four people, most pairs gave each of the four people one cookie, then divided the extra two cookies each into halves, gave each person one of the halves, and then recorded each person's share as $1\frac{1}{2}$. One pair of students began the same way, giving each person one cookie. But then they divided a fifth cookie into four parts and gave each person one of the fourths. They did the same with the sixth cookie, dividing it into fourths and giving each person one of them. They recorded each person's share as $1\frac{2}{4}$. I was happy for the chance to talk about why $\frac{1}{2}$ and $\frac{2}{4}$ represented the same amount. When children have concrete experience with an abstract idea such as this one, it's easier for them to understand and remember what they've learned.

I returned to an activity that was similar to the "close to one-half" activity we did earlier but that required more thinking about fractions. I gave the children a fraction and we talked about whether it was closer to 0, $\frac{1}{2}$, or 1. There was no contest for a fraction like $\frac{7}{8}$ or $\frac{1}{12}$, but $\frac{3}{4}$ caused a lively argument before they agreed that it was halfway between $\frac{1}{2}$ and 1 and therefore the same distance from both. And $\frac{1}{3}$ resulted in a ten-minute argument. Children were trying to figure it out by dividing circles or rectangles into halves and thirds, and the imprecision of their drawings was making for much confusion. It was Daniel who finally gave a convincing argument.

"You know that $\frac{1}{4}$ is halfway between 0 and $\frac{1}{2}$, don't you?" he challenged the class. The others agreed.

"Well, then it's easy," Daniel continued, "because $\frac{1}{3}$ is more than $\frac{1}{4}$. It has to be closer to $\frac{1}{2}$."

Later in the year, I had the students add to their fraction kits, cutting light blue strips into thirds, brown strips into sixths, and pink strips into twelfths. They had to measure carefully for these since folding didn't work as it had for halves, fourths, eighths, and sixteenths. Then the students played Cover Up and Uncover again, making up their own number cubes and deciding which fractions to put on them for a "good" game.

Not everything I did with the students related fractions to real-world experiences or used concrete materials. Sometimes we talked about the fractions by themselves. In these discussions, students would often refer back to situations they had encountered or materials they had used that would help them think about the abstract fractions.

In the spring, I talked with the fifth graders about the canceling-out-zeros rule that was standard when I was taught fractions. I wrote on the board:

$$^{10}/_{20} = {}^1\!/_2$$

"Is this true?" I asked the class. There were murmurs of agreement and several children raised their hands to explain why. By this time in the year, the culture of explaining their reasoning was well entrenched. The children knew I expected explanations and they enjoyed reporting how they thought. I called on Leslie.

"They're the same," she said, "because 10 is half of 20, so $^{10}/_{20}$ is the same as $^1\!/_2$."

Peter had a different way to explain it. He said, "If you had a pizza and you cut it into 20 pieces and then you ate 10 of them, that's the same as eating half of the pizza."

I called on Sarah next. "My reason is kind of like Peter's, but a little different," she said.

"Let's hear it," I said.

She said, "Well, suppose you had two pizzas and you cut one in half and you cut the other into 20 slices. You could put the half of the first pizza on top of the other pizza and it would cover up 10 slices." There were some giggles and comments about the mess this would be.

"But it would prove it," Sarah defended her explanation.

"Does anyone have a different way to explain why $^{10}/_{20}$ is the same as $^1\!/_2$?" I asked to refocus the class.

Eli had been drawing on paper. He looked up and raised his hand. "Can I come up and show?" he said. I nodded. Some students love to come up and draw on the board, and Eli was one of them. He drew a rectangle and divided it in half with a horizontal line.

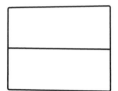

He pointed to the rectangle and said, "See, here's a half and here's a half."

Then he turned back to the board and started to draw vertical lines. I could tell that he was trying to divide the rectangle into 10 vertical sections, and I could also see that he was misjudging the distance between the lines. But I didn't interrupt and we all watched as he drew lines, counted sections, then squeezed in two more lines.

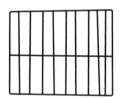

Eli explained, "There are 20 spaces all together, 10 on the top half and 10 on the bottom half. So that shows it."

"Shows what?" I asked, to be sure that Eli could explain how what he had done related to the question I had asked.

"It shows that $^{10}/_{20}$ is the same as $^1/_2$," he said, and returned to his seat.

Everyone seemed to be satisfied that $^{10}/_{20}$ and $^1/_2$ were the same. I then wrote on the board:

$$^{10}/_{40} = {}^1/_4$$

"What about this one?" I asked. "Raise your hand if you think this is true."

A few hands shot up immediately, more followed, and soon almost all were raised. I know that when I ask a question like this in class, peer pressure can be the reason some students raise their hand. That's why the discussion about the answer is very important, so students understand they need to be able to explain why something makes sense, not just say yes or no. And class discussions give students the chance to hear different ways of thinking about ideas.

Again, several students explained why $^{10}/_{40}$ and $^1/_4$ were worth the same, and their explanations were similar to the ones students offered to explain why $^{10}/_{20}$ and $^1/_2$ were the same.

Then I wrote on the board:

$$^{20}/_{30} = {}^2/_3$$

"Raise your hand if you think this one is true," I said.

The room was silent. After a moment, a few hands went up to show agreement, but not many hands followed.

"Hmmm, you don't seem very sure about this one," I said. "Who would like to explain why it is or isn't true?"

"I think it's true," Nick said, "because if you did what Leslie did and cut a pizza into 30 pieces, I think that 20 of the pieces would be $^2/_3$ of the pizza."

"You said you think that's so," I commented. "Are you sure?"

"No, not really," Nick said.

"I'm sure," Leslie said, "because if you had 30 slices, and if you divided the pizza into three big pieces, there would be 10 little slices in each piece, so there would be 20 slices in two pieces, and that's $^2/_3$."

Maria had a different approach. "Suppose you had 30 pennies and you divided them into three equal piles," she said. "Then you'd have a third, a third, and a third." She gestured with her hands to show three imaginary piles. "And there would be 10 pennies in each pile, so in $\frac{2}{3}$ there would be 20 pennies."

"Oh, yeah," Nick said. Maria's explanation seemed to help.

"I can show it my way," Eli volunteered.

Jack groaned. "That takes too long."

"No it won't," Eli protested, "I can use my other drawing. It will take me a minute." Eli looked at me and I nodded. He came to the board and erased the horizontal line carefully, trying not to erase too much of each vertical line. Then he drew two horizontal lines that divided the rectangle into thirds. He turned to the class, grinned, and took a mock bow.

"Who can explain why Eli's drawing shows that $\frac{20}{30}$ is the same as $\frac{2}{3}$?" I asked. I chose Franny. She hadn't volunteered to contribute anything to the discussion yet.

"It's because there are 10 pieces in each row and three rows," Franny said, "so there are 30 pieces, and two of the rows make $\frac{2}{3}$ and that's 20 of the 30 pieces."

I looked at Eli. "That's it," he confirmed.

I then directed the class to the three fraction sentences I had written on the board:

$$\frac{10}{20} = \frac{1}{2}$$
$$\frac{10}{40} = \frac{1}{4}$$
$$\frac{20}{30} = \frac{2}{3}$$

"In the first fraction in each of these," I said, "you can cross out the zero in the numerator and in the denominator and you have the second fraction. When I was in school, we learned this as 'canceling out zeros.'"

"Does it always work?" Sally wanted to know.

"Well, remember when we talked about why a fraction like $\frac{2}{4}$ or $\frac{4}{8}$ is the same as $\frac{1}{2}$?" I asked. The students nodded.

"And remember we talked about how it was okay to divide the numerator and denominator by the same number?" Again, nods.

"Who remembers why that works?" I asked. I waited to give the students a chance to collect their thoughts and then I called on Liza.

"It's okay to multiply or divide them both because it just makes the pieces larger or smaller," she said, "and you're making the top and bottom both larger or smaller. So it works."

David had something to add. "It's like making 6 pizza slices or 8 pizza slices. If you eat half, you eat $3/6$ or $4/8$. It's both the same."

I then explained why canceling the zeros worked. "When you cross out the zero in 20 so it becomes 2, that's the same as dividing 20 by 10. And the same with 30. If you divide 30 by 10, you get 3. So you're dividing the numerator and denominator by the same number."

"So we can do that if we want to?" Erin wanted to know. She often satisfied her need for precision by checking to be sure about what to do.

"As long as what you're doing makes sense to you," I said. "Let's look at this example." I wrote on the board:

$$^{100}/_{200} = {}^1/_2$$

"It's true because 100 is half of 200," Manuel said.

"That's an easy one," Emmy added.

"Look!" Daniel said excitedly. "You cross out the zeros in the ones place and you get 10 over 20. Then you do it again."

"What about this one?" I said. "See if you think it's true." I wrote on the board:

$$^{101}/_{201} = {}^{11}/_{21}$$

"Oooh, that's not easy," Emmy said.

"The numbers are tricky," Leslie said, "but I think it's okay."

The class discussion had been going on for a while and some of the students hadn't contributed. That didn't mean they weren't involved, but it's hard in a whole-class discussion for every student to have the chance to offer an idea. To give more children a chance to verbalize their ideas, I said to the class, "Talk about this at your tables. Then we'll discuss it together."

The groups' conversations were animated. I knew that thinking about this problem was difficult for some of the children. While they can visualize $\frac{1}{2}$, $\frac{2}{3}$, $\frac{10}{20}$, $\frac{20}{30}$, and even $\frac{100}{200}$, it's not easy to visualize $\frac{101}{201}$. It's easy to see that $\frac{101}{201}$ is close to $\frac{1}{2}$, since it's close to $\frac{100}{200}$, but it's not immediately obvious that $\frac{101}{201}$ is larger than $\frac{1}{2}$. (Can you explain why? If you're interested, check problem 6 in the answer key.) It's a little easier to think about or visualize $\frac{11}{21}$. Half of 21 is $10\frac{1}{2}$, and 11 is a little larger, so $\frac{11}{21}$ is also larger than $\frac{1}{2}$.

After three or four minutes, I interrupted the group discussions and called the class to order. There had been a good deal of disagreement, and lots of the students were eager to talk. It was a hard discussion to direct because students were more interested in telling their own ideas than in responding to one another. After each child spoke, I would ask whether anyone had something to ask that person or had a comment to make about his or her idea. If the child I called on started to give a new idea, I'd interrupt and keep the conversation focused on the previous statement. This was hard for lively ten- and eleven-year-olds.

After about fifteen minutes, the class was still divided on the issue, with about the same number in agreement as opposed. Six children in the class weren't committing to either position.

I stopped the conversation. Math class had been going on for about thirty-five minutes.

"Rather than continuing to discuss your ideas," I said to the students, "I'm interested in knowing what each of you thinks. So I'd like you to write down whether or not you think it's true that $\frac{101}{201} = \frac{11}{21}$ and explain why."

The students were used to this sort of request from me. Writing had been a part of math for the entire year, and with the feedback they had gotten from me about using words and numbers, giving sufficient details, and including pictures when it helped, their papers had become enormously useful for giving me insights into how they were thinking and what they understood. Figures 10.1–10.3 are three of the responses I received this time.

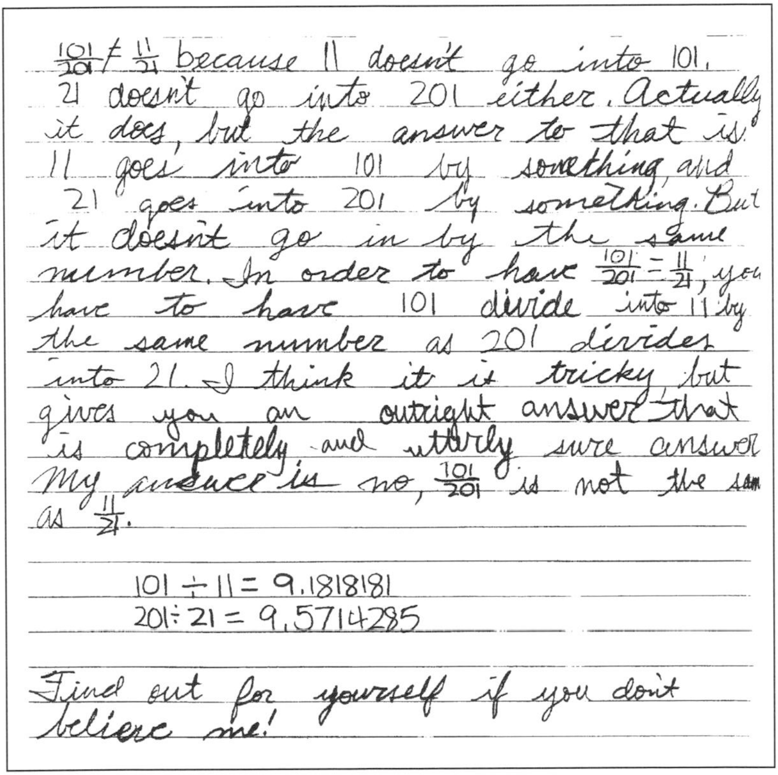

$\frac{101}{201} \neq \frac{11}{21}$ because 11 doesn't go into 101, 21 doesn't go into 201 either. Actually it does, but the answer to that is: 11 goes into 101 by something, and 21 goes into 201 by something. But it doesn't go in by the same number. In order to have $\frac{101}{201} = \frac{11}{21}$, you have to have 101 divide into 11 by the same number as 201 divides into 21. I think it is tricky but gives you an outright answer that is completely and utterly sure answer. My answer is no, $\frac{101}{201}$ is not the same as $\frac{11}{21}$.

$101 \div 11 = 9.1818181$
$201 \div 21 = 9.5714285$

Find out for yourself if you don't believe me!

FIG. 10.1   *Sophia, a fifth grader, explains with certainty why* $^{101}/_{201}$ *is not equal to* $^{11}/_{21}$.

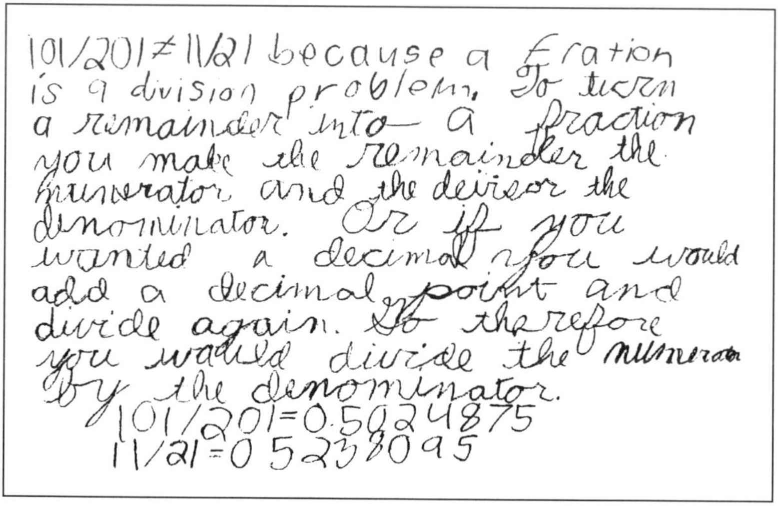

101/201 ≠ 11/21 because a fration
is a division problem. To turn
a remainder into a fraction
you make the remainder the
numerator and the divisor the
denominator. Or if you
wanted a decimal you would
add a decimal point and
divide again. So therefore
you would divide the numerator
by the denominator.
101/201 = 0.5024875
11/21 = 0.5238095

FIG. 10.2   Elissa's paper shows that she understands how fractions and division relate to each other.

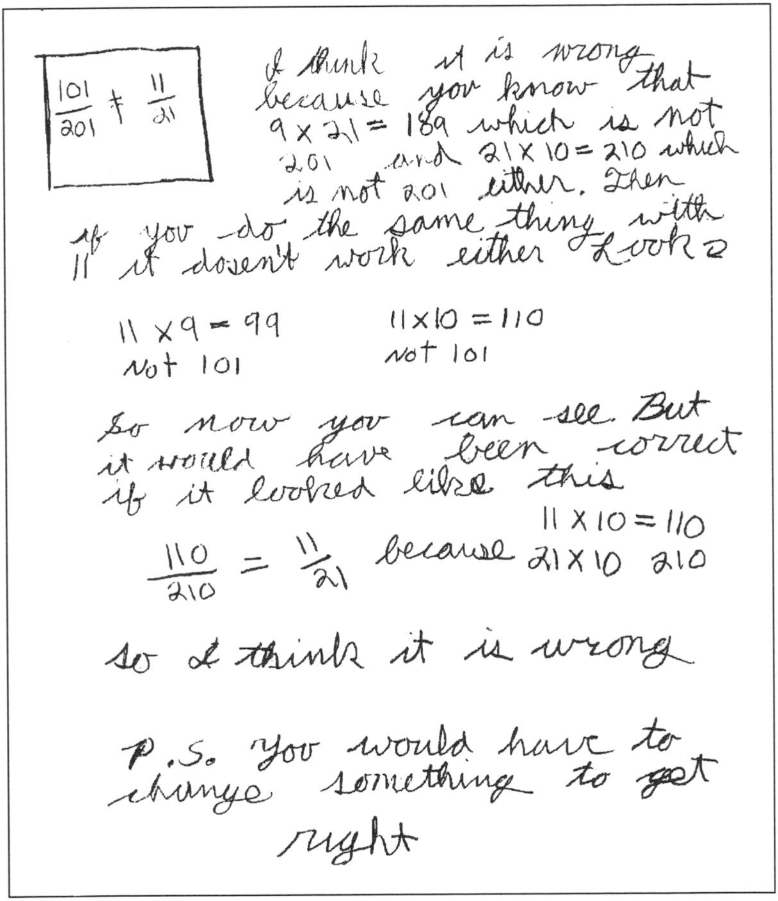

$$\frac{101}{201} \neq \frac{11}{21}$$

I think it is wrong because you know that $9 \times 21 = 189$ which is not 201 and $21 \times 10 = 210$ which is not 201 either. Then if you do the same thing with 11 it dosen't work either Look 2

$11 \times 9 = 99$ $11 \times 10 = 110$
Not 101   Not 101

So now you can see. But it would have been correct if it looked like this

$$\frac{110}{210} = \frac{11}{21}$$ because $\begin{array}{l} 11 \times 10 = 110 \\ 21 \times 10 = 210 \end{array}$

so I think it is wrong

P.S. You would have to change something to get right

FIG. 10.3   *Sarah's explanation is different from those given by the other students.*

To teach children about fractions, I don't have them learn the rules for fractions that we learned when we were in school. That is, I don't teach the rules and then have students practice them; instead, I talk with them about different procedures that make sense.

As I do with whole numbers, I encourage students to figure mentally when appropriate. I expect them to do certain calculations in their head, such as figuring out how much water we'll need if we double a recipe that calls for three-fourths cup or how much ribbon we need to buy if we need a fourth of a yard for each student in the class. For problems like these, I don't want them to rely on pencil and paper, their fraction kit, or any other material. I want them to be able to reason in their head. The emphasis in class is always on making sense, and students are expected to be able to explain the sense in what they are doing.

When I learned fractions, most of the work I did was by myself. That was true for all the math I learned, and for most everything else I learned as well. With these fifth graders, however, the instructional time was split between whole-class instruction, small-group work, and individual assignments, with discussions being a major part of both whole-class instruction and small-group work. For fifth graders, learning math calls for sharing their thinking, listening to others' ideas, asking questions, examining patterns, making conjectures—all for the purpose of bringing meaning to fractions and how we work with them.

Teaching Percents

B y the time they reach eighth grade, students are somewhat familiar with percents. They know that a 50 percent sale means that prices are cut in half and that a 10 percent sale gives a much smaller discount. They've heard on television that some tires have 40 percent more wearing power, that a tennis player gets 64 percent of her first serves in bounds, that there's a 70 percent chance of rain tomorrow. From their prior experience, they've learned that 100 percent represents the whole amount and that 50 percent is half. After that, unless their math instruction emphasized percents in sixth or seventh grade, many students' understanding of them is pretty fuzzy.

Introductory instruction about percents should build on students' existing understanding. It should relate to what students have learned from their prior experiences and extend and broaden their learning. The goal for instruction should be to help students learn to use percents appropriately and effectively in problem situations. That means when students encounter problems with percents, they should be able to arrive at answers by reasoning mathematically, explain why the answers make sense, and make a decision based on the result. Following are descriptions of some lessons I've used to help eighth graders develop the skills they need to work with percents.

To learn more about what the students already knew, I began with an activity called Sense or Nonsense? (Scaaf, et al., *Problem Solving in Mathematics, Grade 7*, Dale Seymour, 1983), in which students are asked to discuss ten statements that incorporate percents.

I planned to have the students work cooperatively on this activity. In class, the students sat in small groups and were accustomed to working together. There were times when they were expected to work individually, of course, but also times when they collaborated. For this lesson, my first direction to them was to take a single sheet of paper for their group and write their names on it.

I had duplicated copies of the ten statements in the activity for each group. But before distributing the statements, I read the first one. It dealt with the idea of 100 percent, an idea familiar to the students:

> Mr. Bragg says he is right 100 percent of the time. Do you think Mr. Bragg is bragging? Why?

Giggles and side comments erupted, and I waited for them to subside before calling on students to respond.

"He's bragging," Adam declared. "No one can be right all the time."

"No one is perfect," Daria added.

"He can't be right every single time, because what about the things he doesn't know?" Beth said.

"If he's always right, then he would be like Albert Einstein," Raul contributed.

After giving all the students a chance to comment, I showed the class the sheet of statements and explained to them what they were to do in their groups.

"For each statement, first have one person in your group read it aloud," I said. "All of you should talk about whether it makes sense or is nonsense. Make sure everyone in your group has a chance to express his or her ideas and then have one person record what you decide and the reasoning behind your decision." The statements presented a variety of situations. For example:

> Rosa has a paper route. She gets to keep 25 percent of whatever she collects. Do you think this is a good deal? Why?

> The "Never Miss" basketball team made 10 percent of the baskets they tried. Do you think they should change their name? Why?

> Ms. Green was complaining. "Prices have gone up at least 200 percent this past year," she said. Do you think she is exaggerating? Why?

"Any questions?" I asked as the groups were about to begin work.

"Should we take turns reading the statements and writing what we think?" Valerie asked.

"Your group can decide the best way to handle the reading and writing," I responded. "It's okay with me if one person does all the reading and one person does all the writing or if you share those jobs, but all of you must get involved and contribute to your group's discussion. Everyone must participate in deciding what you write."

"What if we can't agree?" Jack asked.

"Then you can include the dissenting opinions in what you write on your group paper," I answered.

There were no other questions and the class got to work. The students quickly became engrossed in the activity. I circulated, listening and observing. The students were interested, the groups' discussions were animated, and the time sped by. There were no discipline problems. No groaning. No fear of failing. The assignment was clear and all the students were involved. It's just how math lessons should go. (The papers of three groups are shown in figures 11.1–11.3.)

Sense or Nonsense

(1) Yes ,̂ because nobody's
perfect and 100% of the
time means always.

we agree

(2) Yes its too much, because, 50%
is half so half of $36 is $18.

(3) Our group does not think, its a good deal
because 75% of $1 is 75¢. In two days, Jeff
would already owe more than Joe had
loaned him.

(4) Our group does not think Cindy should
spend 100%, or all of her allowance on
candy.

(5) We agree that the team should change
their name. If they only make 10% of
the baskets, they are missing more than
half the time.

(6) Our group thinks Sarah's score on the
test depends on the number of problems
on the test.

(7) Our group thinks 25% is not enough money
for Rosa to be collecting on her paper route.

(8) Our group believes the forecaster's prediction
is reasonable because in winter it rains
a lot.

(9) We agree Ms. Green was exaggerating
because the most that price could
go up would be 100%

(10) Our group does not believe this is
the "Best Sale Ever" because everything's
only 10% off, which is less than half.

FIG. 11.1   *A small group's explanation of the Sense or Nonsense statements.*

Sense or Nonsense

1) Mr. Bragg is bragging because nobody's perfect and also some questions don't have a right or wrong answer.

2) A 50% tip would be too much because 50% means half and half would 18 dollars. So 18 dollars plus $36 equals $54 and that's too much money.

3) It'll be a pretty good deal for Joe because he only loaned Jeff a dollar and Jeff would have to at least 75¢ more than he borrowed.

4) Cindy spending 100% on candy is not sensible because that is all her money.

5) Yes, they should change their name because "Never miss" means that they never miss and they only make one out of every ten.

6) Doesn't make sense because we don't know how many problems were on the test.

7) Rosa is not getting a good deal because that's only 20¢ per dollar, newspapers only cost 25¢ and she also has to labor and it takes part of her time.

8) It's reasonable because it just rained yesterday.

9) Ms. Green is exaggerating because that's three times as much as the regular price.

10) It's not a good sale because if something costed a dollar before the sale, then you would only get 10¢ off.

FIG. 11.2 *Another small group's explanation of the Sense or Nonsense statements.*

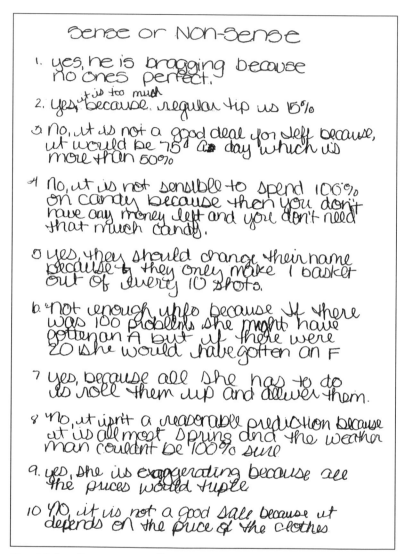

Sense or Non-Sense

1. yes, he is bragging because no ones perfect.

2. yes, because regular tip is 15% *it is too much*

3. no, it is not a good deal for Jeff because, it would be 75¢ a day which is more than 50%

4. no, it is not sensible to spend 100% on candy because then you don't have any money left and you don't need that much candy.

5. yes, they should change their name because they only make 1 basket out of every 10 shots.

6. not enough info because if there was 100 problems she might have gotten an A but if there were 20 she would have gotten an F

7. yes, because all she has to do is roll them up and deliver them.

8. no, it isn't a reasonable prediction because it is almost spring and the weather man couldn't be 100% sure

9. yes, she is exaggerating because all the prices would triple

10. no, it is not a good sale because it depends on the price of the clothes

FIG. 11.3   *One more small group's explanation of the Sense or Non-sense statements.*

The next day, I began class by having groups review what they had written. Then I led a class discussion about the statements. Students were willing to offer their ideas and were interested in hearing what others had to say. There was a heated discussion about the sixth statement on the sheet: *Sarah missed 10 problems on the science test. Do you think her percent is high enough for her to earn an A? Why?* While most of the students were clear that you had to know the number of problems on the test in order to decide, two of the groups argued that missing 10 problems would be okay for earning an A.

"At least she would get an A minus," Josh said.

"Suppose there were only 12 problems on the test," Elissa argued. "How could she get an A then?"

"Oh, yeah," Josh conceded.

I pointed out that a percent describes a relationship between quantities. "Our sales tax is 7 percent," I said, "but that doesn't tell you how much tax you have to pay when you buy something. The amount of tax depends on how much the item costs."

After these discussions of percents in real-world contexts, I taught the students how to calculate percents. Again, I began by building on what the students already knew. And rather than teaching them procedures to use, I kept the emphasis on having them reason in ways that made sense to them and the focus on having them calculate mentally. For this lesson, I used money as the context. Money not only provides a familiar model of our place value system, it's also a topic that always gets eighth graders' attention.

"How much is 50 percent of $100?" I asked the class. Almost everyone's hand shot up. I began with this easy, almost trivial question to establish a reference for what was to come.

"I want to hear your answer, but I'm also interested in your explanation of how you know your answer is correct," I said. I think it's important to be clear with students about what I expect from them. This additional direction not only told the students what their response should include, it also gave the message that

I value their thinking along with correct answers. A few students now became tentative and lowered their hand, but most kept their hand raised.

Patrick answered. "It's $50," he said, "because 50 percent is the same as half of something, and $50 is half of $100." Others nodded, satisfied with Patrick's response. No one offered a different way to explain. I wrote on the board:

50% of $100 is $50

"So, how much is 25 percent of $100?" I asked. Again, many hands went up. I called on Andrea.

"It's $25," she said, "because 25 percent is half of 50 percent, and half of $50 is $25." Again, there were nods.

Josh had a different way of thinking about this. "I just divided $100 four ways and got $25," he said.

"I don't get that," Kim said.

"It's like four quarters in a dollar, but bigger," Josh explained. "There are four $25s in $100." Kim nodded, but I wasn't sure she followed Josh's reasoning. I wrote on the board:

25% of $100 is $25

"What about 10 percent of $100?" I then asked. This time, fewer hands were raised. A minimal response like this lets me know that students aren't confident in their thinking.

"Before I call on anyone to respond," I said, "discuss this in your group." Talking about ideas is a way for students to clarify their thinking, and having them talk in groups gives more students the opportunity to express their ideas. Also, it's easier for some students to express their ideas in small groups than to address the entire class.

I called the class back to attention. "Who would like to explain how to find 10 percent of $100?" I asked. More hands were raised this time. I called on Hiroshi.

"That's $\frac{1}{10}$," he said, "so $\frac{1}{10}$ of $100 is $10."

"How do you know that 10 percent is $\frac{1}{10}$?" I asked Hiroshi. Hiroshi was quiet for a moment. "It just is," he responded. He paused and then added, "I don't know how to explain it." It's not unusual for students to have difficulty explaining their thinking, even when math comes easily to them. Sometimes, students with good mathematical intuitions haven't thought about how to explain their ideas to others. Learning to communicate their understanding is an important part of math learning.

"Who can explain Hiroshi's idea that 10 percent is $\frac{1}{10}$?" I asked the class. As before, only a few students raised their hands, so I again had them talk in their small groups.

After a few minutes I asked the students for their attention, eager to hear what they had to say. There isn't one right way to explain why 10 percent is the same as $\frac{1}{10}$. I was prepared to offer several ways for them to think about this, but first I was interested in hearing their ideas. Listening to students gives me insights into their thinking and is a valuable way for me to assess their understanding.

I called on Susan. She said, "The way I can explain it is that if you add 50 and 50 you get 100, right?"

I nodded.

Susan continued, "So there are two 50 percents in 100 percent, and that makes it half, right?"

Again, I nodded. I wasn't sure where Susan was headed, but I've learned to listen, not interrupt, and give students the chance to develop their reasoning.

"But with 10 percent, you have to add 10 and 10 and 10, like that. You need ten 10s to make 100, so one 10 is $\frac{1}{10}$," Susan concluded.

Conversation broke out in several parts of the room. Since talking about something is a way to make an idea your own, I let the conversations go on for a moment.

"So what do you think?" I asked, finally.

"That was good," Daria said with satisfaction.

"What made it good?"

"It made it clear," Daria responded.

"I liked how she started with the 50 percent," Larry added. "That helped."

"I have a different way to explain it," Josh said.

"Let's hear," I prompted.

"I did it like I did before with the 25 percent and the quarters," he said. "There are ten dimes in a dollar, so a dime is 10 percent of a dollar. So ten $10s makes $100."

"So what do you think?" I again asked the class. No one responded to Josh directly, but there were a few nods.

Then Sarah said in a stage whisper to Manuel, "Tell your idea." We all looked at Manuel. He was a solid thinker and a good group member but he didn't feel comfortable talking to the entire class. He did when prodded, however, and Sarah's request was successful.

"I started with 50 percent like Susan did," he said. "I thought that 50 percent is a half and that's the same as $5/_{10}$. So, then I thought that there are five 10 percents in 50 percent and each of them has to be $1/_{10}$."

"So how much do you think 10 percent of $100 is?" I asked.

"It has to be $10," Manuel said.

"Explain that part," I probed.

"Because there are five 10 percents in 50 percent," he explained. "One of the 10 percents has to be $10 because five of them add up to $50."

I had questioned Manuel further because I was still thinking a bit about Josh's explanation and I needed to shift into how Manuel was thinking. Also, I know that it's often hard to follow someone else's thinking and I felt that additional clarification could be helpful to others in the class.

"Does anyone have a different way to explain why 10 percent of $100 is $10?" I asked. No hands were raised.

"Any other questions about this?" I asked. Again, no hands went up. I wrote on the board:

10% of $100 is $10

"What about 5 percent of $100?" I asked. Most hands shot up. "Let's say the answer softly together," I said, and the class chorused, "Five dollars."

"That's easy," Valerie explained. "It's half of 10 percent."

"What about one percent of $100?" I asked. It took a moment for most hands to go up. Again, the class answered in a chorus, and Beth followed up with an explanation. Now I had recorded on the board:

50% of $100 is $50
25% of $100 is $25
10% of $100 is $10
5% of $100 is $5
1% of $100 is $1

I then wrote on the board:

50% of $200 is _____
25% of $200 is _____
10% of $200 is _____
5% of $200 is _____
1% of $200 is _____

I gave the class directions. "Each of you copy these into your notebook and figure out the answers on your own," I said. "Try to think of more than one way you can do each calculation. Then talk in your groups about how to explain the answers. We'll have a class discussion afterward."

The strategies they reported in the class discussion were generally similar to the ways they had figured for $100. However, there were some differences as well.

In explaining why 25 percent of $200 was $50, for example, Kim reported, "I knew that 50 percent of $200 was $100, so half of that is $50."

Raul, however, had a different explanation. "I doubled $25," he said, "because I knew that 25 percent of $100 was $25, and $200 is the double of $100."

Hiroshi explained, "I know that four 50s make 200," he said, "so 25 percent of 200 is $50." Hiroshi could tell that I was about to ask him for further explanation and he hastily added, "It works because 25 percent is ¼."

For homework, I asked the students to make the same chart as I had for $200, but to substitute other amounts—$500, $80, and $75. I knew that $500 and $80 would be fairly easy for the students. Figuring with $75 might be a challenge for some of them, but their answers to $80 could serve as a useful reference.

The next day in class, I had the students compare their homework answers in their groups and then raise questions about those on which they had disagreed. Then we continued by mentally calculating other percentages—60 percent, 75 percent, 15 percent, 30 percent, 95 percent, and so on. For each, the students built on what they already knew, which helped them not only cement their previous learning but extend it.

So far I had chosen numbers that were fairly easy to work with; I didn't want complicated calculations to make understanding more difficult. But more often than not the world presents us with problems that involve "messy" numbers, and it's important for students to learn to apply their understanding to all amounts, not just to tidy amounts like $100 or $200. We did many investigations with messy numbers.

One such investigation had to do with left-handed people. A *Newsweek* survey had reported that 12 percent of Americans are left-handed, and I built a lesson around this statistic. At the beginning of class one day, I posted a sheet of chart paper titled Are You Right-Handed or Left-Handed? I ruled two columns, labeling them Left-Handed and Right-Handed, and asked the students to sign their name in the correct column. We collected statistics on class charts like this one often during the year, and then we'd analyze and graph the data.

After collecting our class's left-handed/right-handed data, I planned to have the students analyze how it compared to the average reported in *Newsweek*. Then we'd use *Newsweek's* 12 percent average to estimate the number of left-handed students in the entire school. Finally, we'd do a school tally and check to see how our school actually compared with the national percentage.

There were 28 students in class that day and 3 of them indicated that they were left-handed. I gave the class the statistic about left-handed people. Then I said, "So how does our class compare to the statistic that 12 percent of Americans are left-handed? Before I ask you to work on this in your groups, let's talk about it first. What ideas do you have?"

Having a class discussion first raises a broader range of ideas than individuals or groups typically have on their own. When I was in school, a discussion like this was usually avoided because it might "give away" the answer. But since students have to include explanations of the answers they decide on, this doesn't bother me. Students can't explain what they don't understand, and discussions can help spark their thinking. Besides, class lessons are designed for learning, not as tests of what children can do. Making errors and being unsure or confused are natural parts of learning, and class lessons ought to give as much support as possible to students when they are in the process of forming new understanding.

"We have to figure out what percent of us is left-handed," Josh said.

"No kidding," Nick said sarcastically. I shot Nick a look that made him realize that his comment was out of line.

"Sorry, Josh," he said. Josh didn't respond.

"We don't have to figure out what percent of us is left-handed, I don't think," Daria said. "We could figure out how much of us . . . I mean, how many of us . . . is 12 percent."

"I don't get it," Jack said.

Andrew looked up. "I think it's less," he said.

"What's less?" Hiroshi asked.

"I think that we don't have enough left-handers," Andrew said.

"What do you mean by 'we don't have enough left-handers'?" I asked.

"We don't have 12 percent. I figured out we only have about 10 percent," Andrew said.

"How did you do that?" Susan asked.

"I figured that 28 people is close to 30 people," Andrew explained. "Three out of 30 people is the same as $\frac{1}{10}$, and that's 10 percent."

Students began talking about what Andrew had said. Several got out paper and pencil and started to figure. My plan to have a discussion and then have them work in their groups was being preempted by Andrew's statement, but that was fine with me. The discussion was going well, the students were engaged, and this was just as good a way to talk about the mathematics involved. After some more talk, the consensus was that about 10 percent of the students in this class were left-handed.

"Why do you think our class statistic is different from the national statistic?" I asked.

"No one asked us," Nick blurted out, then looked at me to be sure he wasn't out of line again.

"They can't ask everyone in the country when they do a survey," Elissa said. "They use a sample." When learning about statistics earlier in the year, we had talked about the idea that data from a sample were often sufficient for describing a larger population.

"We're close, anyway," Beth added.

"Who do you think is concerned about what percentage of the American population is left-handed?" I asked.

"Left-handed people!" Patrick said. The others laughed. Patrick was one of the left-handed students.

"What about baseball players?" Andrew asked. "Left-handed people make good pitchers."

"That's because most of the batters are right-handed," Adam said.

"So the manufacturers of fielders' gloves need the information," I said. "It can help them decide how many right-handed and left-handed gloves to manufacture."

"For golf clubs, too," Susan said.

"And scissors," Patrick added.

I then posed a problem for the students to work on in their

groups. "There are about 500 students in our school," I said to them. "How many of our students do you think are left-handed?"

"How will we know if we're right?" Daria asked.

"Do you mean how will you know if your calculation is correct or how will you know if that's the number of left-handed students in school?" I asked.

"Well, both, I guess," Daria answered.

"Can we take a poll?" Valerie asked.

"That would be cool!" Larry said.

I had anticipated that the students would be intrigued by the idea of conducting a poll, and I was prepared with a list of the homeroom classes and their teachers. I planned to divide this list among the students and have them write letters asking the homeroom teachers to report back the total number of students in their class and the number who were left-handed. The letters would explain why the information was needed and promise to let the teachers know the schoolwide results.

Projects like this can eat up a teacher's time, but they're worth it, both because students are eager to do them and because they get students thinking about percents by analyzing real statistical data.

But first, the students figured out how much 12 percent was of 500 students. They did this in various ways.

Adam wrote: *Out of 100, 12% would be 12 people. Since 500 is 5 × more than 100, you times 12 × 5 = 60.*

Susan wrote: *10% is 50 people and 1% is 5 people. You add 50 and 5 and 5 and you get 60 people.*

Elissa's method was similar to Susan's. She wrote: *10% of 500 is 50 people, 1% of 500 is 5 people, 2% is 10 people. So 12% is 50 people plus 10 people, which is 60 people.*

From time to time, I brought in real-life situations I had been collecting that presented percent problems. For example, a coupon for a fast-food restaurant offered 70 cents off the regular price ($3.59) of a hamburger, fries, and a large drink. I had students figure out what percent discount the coupon gave them.

An advertisement from a newspaper showed a pair of earrings, listing the sale price of $36.40 and the regular price of $52.00. The students figured what percent discount this was. Another advertisement offered a 20 percent savings on various household items and students figured the sale price for them.

Sometimes I asked the students to work individually first and then talk in their groups. Other times they'd talk in their groups first and then write individual papers. Occasionally we'd talk as a class first before they did either individual or group work. I mixed it up, depending on the problem, on whether I needed to assess them individually, and on whether I thought the group interaction was needed to support their learning.

We talked about how to figure the sales tax on discounted items. I asked students if the sales tax on a sale item should be figured on the original price first and then the discount should be taken, or if it was okay to figure the sales tax on the discounted amount. "Would you pay more one way or the other, or does it not matter?" I asked them.

"How much was the discount?" Jack asked.

"I didn't have a particular discount in mind," I said. "Use any price and any discount."

"Then it doesn't matter what sales tax you use either," Andrew said.

"How come?" Kim asked.

"Because it's just like a test case," Andrew answered. "Make your figuring easier."

"Okay, that makes sense," Kim said.

The sales tax problem was a complicated one, I thought, and I had them work in groups. Beth, Susan, Jack, and Hiroshi wrote: *It doesn't matter because it comes out the same. A certain number minus the discount plus the tax equals the same as if you minus the tax then plus the discount.*

Andrew, Daria, Adam, and Valerie wrote: *We preferred to do the discount first then the sales tax because it seems you would be going backwards. But it doesn't matter which one you do first because it comes to the same amount. But if you do the discount first you have an approximation on how much you're paying.*

(Do you agree with these students? Check problem 7 in the answer key if you want an explanation of why they are correct.)

And these students dove into the copier problem I mentioned in chapter 3, the chapter about tip tables. The original square I had duplicated measured 5 inches on a side; one of the reductions I gave the groups measured 3.5 inches on a side. To explain how they figured out that it was a 70 percent reduction, one group wrote: *The 5 inch square is 100%. 5 ÷ 100 = 20%. So one inch equals 20%. 3.5 times 20 is 70. So it was a 70% reduction.*

Another group's solution was similar: *If 5 inches is 100%, that means 1 inch is 20% and ½ inch is 10%. You add 20% + 20% + 20%, and that's 60% and that's 3 inches, and then you add on 10% more. It's 70%.*

Most of the other groups gave variations on these responses. One group, however, did three calculations:

$$3.5 \times 5 = 17.50$$
$$3.5 \div 5 = .70$$
$$5 \div 3.5 = 1.42$$

They wrote: *Since the copy is smaller the only answer that makes sense is 70%.*

While the solution of the students in this last group shows their uncertainty about approaching the problem, the way they arrived at the answer shows a kind of mathematical ingenuity. This kind of information isn't available to teachers when students provide only answers to math problems and not their thinking about how they arrived at them.

Uncertainty is an indication of partial understanding, and partial understanding and confusion are natural parts of the process of learning. In this instance, these students got the correct answer of 70 percent. But when understanding isn't robust, it's more typical for children to make mistakes. Mistakes, however, aren't catastrophes. They are opportunities for learning. Students shouldn't be made to feel deficient when they don't understand something yet.

When helping students develop new understanding and new skills, it's important to keep in mind that learning happens over time and that children learn on different schedules. While some of the eighth graders learned quickly and easily how to work with percents, others needed more time. That's fine. The goal of instruction should be to help children learn in ways that pay attention to who they are, what they know, and how they best learn. Only with that approach to math instruction can we be effective in helping students become competent math learners, stay interested and involved with math, and avoid developing math phobia.

A Message
to Parents

Parents are concerned about their children's math learning. That's good. But many parents also feel insecure about how to help. That's not so good.

While at an art center reception recently, I was chatting with a journalist for *The New York Times*. When I mentioned I was writing a book, she asked what it was about.

"It's about why what was good enough for us in math teaching isn't good enough for our children," I answered.

"Isn't that the truth," she responded. She confided the difficulties she'd had learning math and told me that her poor math ability has always been a serious hindrance. "I actually had to search for a college that didn't require that I take any math," she said. "There was a science requirement, but I took an astronomy course for nonscience majors that got me through."

She worried about her children. "My older boy seems to enjoy math," she said, "but I'm worried that I won't be able to help him with his math homework."

"How old are your children?" I asked.

"The older is six and the younger is three," she said.

"So the homework your older child will be bringing home is first-grade work," I said.

She laughed. "Yes, I guess it will be all right for a while, but I worry that I won't be able to understand the math later on."

I've met many parents who are similarly burdened by a fear about mathematics. That's what a phobia is—a persistent fear of something. While it's a very common feeling about mathematics, it's much less prevalent in relation to reading. Parents are also concerned about their children's learning to read, but they face their concern with direct action. They read with their children, and typically enjoy doing so. They like the closeness that story time produces. They feel good about giving their children a positive experience with reading and helping them learn to appreciate books. They understand the benefits to their children.

It's been documented that the time parents spend reading with their children clearly has a positive and lasting effect on their children's reading success. This makes sense. There's no substitute for the influence that loving attention can have on children's learning.

So it also makes sense that this same kind of loving attention from parents would go a long way to support children's math learning. It's important to give children the kind of attention that will start them learning math when they're young, start them learning math in the right way. This sort of attention to math is sorely lacking, not because parents are uninterested and unconcerned, but because parents claim they don't know how to contribute. They value the importance of math, but they don't see it as a subject they can enjoy with their children. For many parents, learning math was a nightmare, and they haven't a clue about how to offer their children another viewpoint or give them a more positive experience.

If you're among the clueless, here are some beginning tips. They don't require that you go back to school and learn more math, but they do require that you undertake some attitude adjustment.

Tip 1
Don't pass on a negative math attitude to your children.

Let's have none of this "I hate math," "I was never any good in math," "Math was my worst subject," "Grandpa wasn't any good at math, either," "You just have to struggle and do it," or any such comment. None of these help your child.

I'm not asking you to tell your children things that aren't true. If you didn't like math, you didn't. If you did poorly in math at school, that was that. But offering up that information won't support your child. Quite the opposite, it can convince your child that he or she won't be able to do math, or provide an easy excuse for not even trying.

A much better attitude to convey is one of curiosity. "Let's look at that together." "I'm not sure I remember that, but if we can't figure it out, we'll ask for help." "Tell me what you learned about this so far." "Boy, you're learning things I never learned. Let's work on it together."

Get the idea? You've got to say things that don't bash math, that hint at a healthy curiosity about math, and that point toward learning together.

Tip 2
Let your children see you doing math.

You do plenty of mathematical thinking and reasoning each day; there are plenty of opportunities for your children to see you using math. I'm not talking about balancing your checkbook and grumbling about it the entire time. Hey, let's think about times you do math when it serves a useful purpose and is actually a positive, perhaps even fun, experience. No negativity allowed.

You can't think of any times you use math in this way? Try a little harder. Think of things you do in a given day—digging in your wallet or pocket for change to pay for a purchase, figuring out when you need to leave the house to get to the movies on time, choosing the right-size bowl for the leftover spaghetti, measuring the plant food into the watering can when you feed your houseplants, measuring ingredients when you whip up something in the kitchen. Getting any ideas yet? How about keeping score when you're playing bridge (or some other game), being sure there are plates and silverware for everyone when you set the table, centering a picture on the wall between the windows, cutting the pie for dessert so that everyone gets a piece? The problem may be that you haven't realized that you do math every day!

But now that you have some ideas, when your children are around, do the mathematical thinking out loud. Let them hear you figure out the time you need to leave to get to the movies on time. Talk out loud about which measuring cup or spoon you need when you're cooking. Count change out loud when you're paying for something at the cash register.

And remember, no complaining. No emotional charge. Just thinking mathematically, a natural part of living.

Tip 3
Involve your child in doing math.

There are two parts to this tip. One is a direct line from tip 2. Include your children when you're doing math. Let them figure out how much admission will be for all of you at the movies, choose which measuring spoons to use for three-quarters of a teaspoon of salt, decide how many soft drinks you'll need for the party, help you measure the wood for a do-it-yourself bookcase, figure out how much you owe the baby-sitter. I know these things usually take more time when your child helps, but consider the time a valuable investment in your child's mathematical future.

The second part of tip 3 asks you to think about the pleasure you have reading with your child, cuddling in a chair together, close, warm, and loving. You know how your child loves to read the same book over and over, often catching you if you skip a word or reciting from memory as you turn the page. The good news here is that there are a growing number of wonderful books for young children that deal with mathematics—not just counting books, but engaging stories that will help your child learn to love reading while also sparking an interest in math. And many of them include suggestions for how you can extend the stories and engage your child in thinking about and doing mathematics. You may find yourself learning some things about mathematics that weren't part of the traditional curriculum when you were in school, things having to do with geometry, measurement, patterns, probability, and statistics. Check with your librarian or at your local bookstore.

There's no one right or best way to support math learning, or any learning, for that matter. You'll have to tinker with what works for you and for your children. But doing nothing has zero chance of helping, and that's a math concept we all understand.

Solving the Phobia Problem

CHAPTER 13

Since I decided to write this book, my math-phobia antennae have become extremely sensitive. Here are a few things I've heard and read recently that have caught my attention.

▼ *USA Today* regularly includes statistical looks at our nation. On June 26, 1997, the featured question was, "Are students ready for work?" The survey compared the opinions of high school seniors with those of employers about whether students were prepared in various job skills. The categories included working in diverse groups, oral communication, written communication, ability to meet deadlines, basic computer skills, and, you guessed it, basic math skills. While 62 percent of students thought they were "very well" prepared in basic math skills, only 8 percent of employers felt they were. That's quite a discrepancy. And students without basic math skills are at considerable risk in the job market. Page 4 of *Everybody Counts*, the National Research Council report to the nation on the future of mathematics education, states: "Over 75 percent of all jobs require proficiency in simple algebra and geometry, either as a prerequisite to a training program or as part of a licensure examination."

▼ In May 1994, the American Psychiatric Association published the fourth edition of the *Diagnostic and Statistical Manual of Mental Disorders (DSM-IV)*. Psychiatrists and clinical psychologists across the country use this manual to diagnose disorders. The handbook's coding system is used on patient records and on invoices to insurance companies. Mathematics Disorder is in the manual, code 315.1. (It hasn't always been there. It was introduced in the third edition [1980] as Developmental Arithmetic Disorder, and was changed to Mathematics Disorder in the fourth edition.) Disorders in this section of the manual are usually first evident in childhood or adolescence, but they occasionally are not diagnosed until adulthood. The description of Mathematics Disorder states: "Mathematics ability, as measured by individually administered standardized tests, is substantially below that expected given the person's chronological age, measured intelligence, and age-appropriate education." It goes on to say that this disorder "significantly interferes with academic achievement or activities of daily living that require mathematical ability."

▼ In 1997 the Dreyfus Corporation, in collaboration with the National Center for Women and Retirement Research, conducted a Gender Investment Comparison Study, interviewing 415 men and 872 women between the ages of eighteen and eighty whose average household income was $30,000 or more. Here's some of what the study found:

• Adult women have significantly lower levels of math comfort than their male counterparts.

• Those with low math comfort are more risk averse, less apt to make investment decisions, fearful of those they do make, and less financially prepared for retirement.

• Only 41 percent of male respondents and 28 percent of female respondents claim to be comfortable with their high school math skills.

• By conquering math anxiety early in life, Americans are more likely to invest intelligently later on, increase their fi-

nancial knowledge and worth, and establish a more secure retirement.
- Respondents who feel comfortable with math in the present are less likely to put off financial decisions for fear of making a mistake.

While this information all points quite handily to our rampant problem with mathematics, it doesn't do so with the emotional punch of the personal stories I've heard.

On a plane trip to Minneapolis last spring, I read *Durable Goods*, a novel by Elizabeth Berg (Avon Books, 1993). Ever since my conversations with the Boeing engineer on my flight to Seattle (which you can read about in chapter 3 on tip tables and chapter 6 on calculators), I've stopped having conversations with airplane seatmates about mathematics. Now when I fly I take a break from math and read for pleasure, and Elizabeth Berg's book is a gem of a coming-of-age novel. It's the story of Katie, twelve years old, whose mother has recently died and whose father, an army colonel, is raising her and her older sister on an army base in rural Texas. The book has nothing to do with mathematics, or so I thought when I began.

Early in the story, Katie lies to her father about not having any homework to do that day: "Well, I lied about no homework and so I must do my math by flashlight under my covers. The long division makes me cry. First, I put down six, and that's too much. Then I put down five, and that's too little. Then I put down six, and that's too much. I erase and erase, make holes in the paper."

I didn't do more than note the reference, reading on, carried along by the unfolding of the story. Katie's best friend, Cherylanne, lives next door, and Cherylanne's mother, Belle, is a wonderfully nurturing person in Katie's life. Later in the novel, Katie and Belle are baking. Belle is being patient and gentle about helping Katie learn how to break eggs without getting the shells mixed in. Katie notices: "I'd been taught tenderly, and that's how a lesson stays. . . . It's so easy to go the other way. One of the reasons I have trouble with math is that the teacher punishes you for being wrong. When you miss too much, he draws a circle on the blackboard just above the level of your nose, and then tells you to put your nose in it. Naturally you have to be on tiptoe to do it. He has you stay there till your leg muscles feel shaky. He divided our class up the third week of school into smart, middle, and dumb groups. All that trouble I have with numbers this year, that's all Mr. Hornman's.'"

So much for an airplane trip without thinking about mathematics.

When I began to write this book, I read an article about Berg in *The Boston Globe*. I contacted her, telling her not only that I enjoyed her writing but that I was writing a book about math phobia and was struck by her vivid and disturbing references in *Durable Goods* to learning math.

"I was terrible in math," Berg told me. "I hated it and I still have an aversion to numbers. I had such a bad start as an army brat changing schools often, and math was always my weakness."

The stories in the book were true, Berg said, and she related several others equally horrible. "But I had a teacher for algebra who didn't get exasperated with me," Berg remembered. "He had patience and gave me one-on-one help. He went over and over things until I would understand. I started with a C, then I went to B, and finally to an A. It was because of his kindness and interest. But today I still have a physical reaction to math and can feel my stomach tighten whenever I have to deal with numbers. There's no richness in numbers for me; there's richness in ideas, but not in numbers. And I'm very definitely limited now as an adult because of this."

Scores of people have told me of a similar aversion to math, about their fear, dismay, anxiety, avoidance, dislike, inadequacy, incapability, and more. I've heard it all, a heap of personal descriptions that add up to a national phobia.

There is only one way that people can conquer their problem with mathematics: get involved with mathematics and learn more about it. Knowledge is power, it's been said, and here's a situation where knowledge can help, for sure. There are emotional roots that impact the problem, but knowledge is what's needed.

So, what's a possible national solution? Have everyone start learning math again in ways that provide support, encouragement, even pleasure?

Well, why not? Let's take the bull by the horns, in a mathematical way, and use the very self-reliance that helped build our country. Let's all start learning together.

I'm not kidding. I'm interested in other suggestions and open to them. A great deal of effort will be needed to make a difference. But here's one suggestion to get the ball rolling. Let's bring our collective intelligence to the wonder of mathematics and make some progress together.

We can do it. What we need is a national mathematics learning campaign—a national call to action. We'll all look at mathematical problems together, talk about solutions, discover mathematical relationships, make mathematical connections, get help from those who have more experience and knowledge, and all advance. We'll begin to build a nation of lifelong learners of mathematics.

This could happen. It would require the effort and involvement of lots of people. But it's doable. Let's get the cereal makers involved and put on the backs of cereal boxes engaging ways to think about math so families can start their mornings with breakfast and math. Let's get radio talk show hosts to do some daily talking about mathematics, maybe the way *Car Talk* on National Public Radio does with its weekly puzzlers. Let's get all the late-night TV show hosts to include at least one good math problem in their opening monologues and invite audience participation. Let's get movie theaters to devote a bit of preshow screen time to some good math. Maybe we need a Broadway show: *Math—The Musical*. Let's get the on-line services to offer up a math problem a day with a chat room for discussing it. Let's get Madison Avenue advertising agencies on this. Let's get the ball rolling.

I know. You can't imagine math problems interesting enough

to catch people's interest. Math just isn't sexy enough, you think. You probably skipped the problems that you've already read in this book, or looked ahead to the answer key to get the agony over with. Math just can't sell, you think.

Okay, math isn't your thing. But you've gotten this far in this book. I'm willing to say you just haven't had your interest and imagination caught *yet*. Let me try out a possible idea for a national math campaign that could begin to mobilize the nation mathematically.

Let's have a national contest—a national $1.00 word search.

Here's how it would work. To figure out if a word is worth $1.00, you add up the values of its letters, with $a = \$.01$, $b = \$.02$, $c = \$.03$, and so on up to $z = \$.26$. If you took the word *math*, for example, it's worth $\$.42$ because the m is worth $\$.13$, the a is worth $\$.01$, the t is worth $\$.20$, and the h is worth $\$.08$. That's $\$.42$. Not enough. *Mathematics* won't work either. It's worth $1.12, too much. Neither of these words could be entries in the contest.

But try *inflation*. Now there's a solid $1.00 word. Really. (Check it out for yourself if you don't trust me.) And there are lots of other $1.00 words. I know of more than 500 in the English language, and I'm sure there are others.

Searching for $1.00 words is an activity that requires being interested in words and being willing to add. Remember, there are three ways you can do the adding part—in your head, with paper and pencil, or on a calculator or computer. Maybe language buffs can help with strategies, figuring out the value of common suffixes, like *ing* or *ed*, and then keeping them in mind when looking for $1.00 words. Maybe we could have spin-off contests looking for the longest $1.00 word, the shortest.

For an advanced spin-off, we could ask for submissions of $1.00 sentences—sentences in which every word is worth $1.00. Here's a nine-word example: *Whenever Henrietta whistled, thirty trembling costumed elephants merrily performed.*

Or we could ask people to submit proofs of $1.00 theorems, such as: *A $1.00 word has to have at least five letters.*

Not impressed with this contest idea? Not even interested in searching for $1.00 words?

Well, okay, I don't really think that a $1.00 word contest is going to be the cure for our national phobia. There's no quick and easy cure for decades of poor attitudes and limited success. But not doing anything certainly won't help. We have to start somewhere. We need to change how we think about and relate to mathematics. Our children deserve nothing less.

Not Your Everyday
Answer Key

I t's difficult to follow someone else's reasoning. That's why it's hard to learn mathematics merely by listening to other people's explanations. Listening isn't enough. You have to turn those ideas around in your own head in order to make sense of them for yourself.

The same is true for reading mathematical explanations. Merely reading isn't enough. You have to think about each idea. Also, it helps to write things down when you're reading mathematics, to keep track of your reasoning. And when you can, it's a good idea to make sketches.

This answer key for the seven math problems posed in this book is different from those in most math books: some of the answers here are long-winded explanations. That's because a correct answer alone is not enough information to reveal the mathematical reasoning behind the answer, and the goal of these answers is to help you think mathematically, not merely let you know whether you're right or wrong. The answers attempt to explain the mathematics that underlies thinking about the problems. So, as you read them, have paper and pencil at hand to help you keep track of the explanation.

Problem 1
(from chapter 2)

Draw a square. Then draw a square that has twice the area. How do the lengths of the sides of the two squares compare?

This problem came up when I was thinking about how I'd know when a ball of rising pizza dough had doubled in size. I made the problem simpler by thinking about how I'd know when a square doubled in area. I drew a square and then I drew a square with its sides twice as long; the area of the larger square was four times the area of the original square.

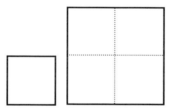

This convinced me that a square with an area twice as large as another square can't have sides that are twice as long. The sides of the larger square have to be shorter in order for the area only to double. The question is: how long should the sides be on the larger square?

One way to approach this is by trial and error. Trial and error is a perfectly respectable method for solving problems. It's not always the most efficient method, but it can be useful.

Okay, how about a square with sides 1½ times as long. Is its area twice as much?

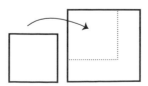

Well, it's closer than my first try, for sure, but it's still too big. It's too big by that little square in the bottom corner, which is $\frac{1}{9}$ of the area of the larger square.

I could keep using trial and error, honing in on the correct-size square, but I don't think that's the best approach. It's not very elegant, some mathematicians would say. But at least trial and error helped me realize that the sides of the larger square need to be a little less that $1\frac{1}{2}$ times the sides of the original square.

Here's another way to think about the problem. Suppose I drew a 10-by-10 grid inside the original square.

It now has 100 teensy squares in it. A square with half the area would have 50 teensy squares inside. I know that 7×7 is 49, which is very close to 50. So, if I drew a 7-by-7 square, using those teensy squares, it would have an area of 49 teensy square units.

Oops, I'm going the wrong way. That gets me a smaller square with half the area. How can I draw a larger one with twice the area?

I know. Instead of drawing a 10-by-10 grid inside the original square, I could draw a 7-by-7 grid in it; the area of the square would be 49 square units. Then I could use the same-size units to draw a 10-by-10 square, which would have an area of 100 square units. That would almost work. The larger square would have an area that is twice as much—plus two square units extra. Pretty close. But I think we can get closer. Besides, it's hard to draw a 7-by-7 grid inside a square.

New thought. Imagine that on top of the original square I place another square the same size. And imagine that I cut the square on top into four triangles.

Now I flip each of the four triangles.

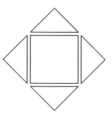

After flipping back the four triangles, the new shape is a square. It's on the diagonal, so you have to tilt your head. Or rotate the shape. Try it and you'll see that you now have a square that is made from two of the original squares. That's it. Hurray! Maybe you can think of another way, but at least that's one that works.

Now, how can I find out how long the side of the twice-as-large square is? One way is to think about the original square as having sides that are one unit long. Then its area is 1 × 1, or one square unit. The new square has an area of two square units, so you have to find a number that gives you 2 when you multiply it by itself. That's the square root of 2. (A square root of a number is another number that you multiply by itself to get the first number.) You can find out what the square root of 2 is on your calculator. (Well, you can come pretty close.) Press 2 and √ (the square root key) and the display on your calculator will show something like 1.4142135. If you multiply that number by itself, the answer will be 1.9999998 or something very close to that, which will be as close to 2 as you can get since there isn't any number that you can represent on a calculator that will produce an exact answer of 2 when you multiply it by itself. The square root of 2 is an irrational number.

But, remember, if you don't know about irrational numbers, you can solve the problem by drawing squares on a piece of paper and then cutting them out. This is a fine way to solve the problem. Even elegant.

Problem 2
(from chapter 3)
The cover of this book measures 5½ inches by 8¼ inches. I drew a rectangle that size and reduced it on my copier machine. Then I reduced it again using the same percentage. And then I reduced it a third time, again using the same percentage. The rectangle below is the result. What percent reduction do you think I used? Could I have gotten the same-size rectangle with two equal reductions? two unequal reductions?

You can get the reduced rectangle by making three reductions at 75 percent. You can also get the reduced rectangle by making two reductions at 65 percent each. Using two unequal percentages, there are various solutions. For example, you can make a reduction at 70 percent followed by a reduction at 60 percent (if your machine lets you go that low).

I started by measuring the dimensions of the reduced rectangle. It's about $2\frac{5}{16}$ inches wide and about $3\frac{1}{2}$ inches long.

Let's talk first about the three-reduction version of the problem. I used trial and error. I picked 80 percent as a starting point, then multiplied 8.25 by 80 percent and got 6.6. (I did this by pressing 8.25, then the × key, then 80, and then the % key. If my calculator didn't have a % key, I would have pressed 8.25, then the × key, then .8, and then the = key.) Then I multiplied 6.6 by 80 percent and got 5.28, and finally I multiplied 5.28 by 80 percent and got 4.224. So using a reduction of 80 percent three times, the resulting rectangle would have a length of 4.224 inches, which is about 4¼ inches. But the length of the reduced rectangle was only 3½ inches, so I had to reduce it more.

Next I tried 70 percent. Again, I multiplied 8.25 by 70 percent and got 5.775; I multiplied 5.775 by 70 percent and got 4.0425; finally I multiplied 4.0425 by 70 percent and got 2.82975. Oops, that's less than 3 inches. That's too much of a reduction.

So I tried 75 percent. I multiplied three times and wound up with 3.4804687 inches. Close enough to 3½ inches for me, I figured.

I checked 75 percent on the other dimension—5½ inches. I multiplied 5.5 by 75 percent, then the answer by 75 percent, and then that answer by 75 percent again. The result: 2.3203125. Hmmm, how does that compare to 2⁵⁄₁₆ inches? I converted ⁵⁄₁₆ to a decimal by dividing 5 by 16 and that's .3125, so 2⁵⁄₁₆ is 2.3125. Again, close enough to satisfy me.

For the second part of the problem, to figure it in only two reductions, I used trial and error again. I knew that I'd have to get a smaller reduction the first time than I did with the 75 percent reduction, so I fiddled around and found out that 65 percent works: 8.25 times 65 percent is 5.3625, and that times 65 percent gives 3.485625. Bingo. And it checks out on the width as well.

Whenever I need to make reductions or enlargements of copies, I confess that I most often use trial and error at the machine, entering a percentage and seeing what results. It's not terribly efficient, but I've gotten good at making reasonable first estimates. That comes from thinking about problems like the one I presented to you and from the experience I have at the copier. (Teachers use copier machines quite often.) So I can rely on my intuition and fall back on some computation. Either way works.

Problem 3
(from chapter 5)

Which is the better buy of hand lotion—a 16-ounce container that costs $3.49 or a 20-ounce container that costs $4.39?

It turns out that the smaller container is a slightly better buy! Not by much, however. The way I came to this conclusion was to figure out the price per ounce for each size. Since 16 ounces cost $3.49, I wondered what one ounce would cost. I divided $3.49 by 16 and got $.218125. For the larger size, I divided $4.39 by 20 and got $.2195. Then I subtracted to find the difference. The larger container costs $.001375 per ounce more than the smaller. And that's not worth talking about—both cost about 22 cents an ounce.

I did this figuring at home with paper, pencil, and a calculator. I checked my work by doing it again. I'm sure I'm right.

But I still wondered whether I could have come to that conclusion when I was in the drugstore without paper, pencil, or a calculator. How could I have figured this out in my head?

I talked with my friend Sandra about this, and she had an idea that helped me. (It's often useful to talk with someone about problems. Other points of view can be awfully helpful.)

Suppose the 16-ounce size were enlarged to a 20-ounce size but kept at the same price-per-ounce cost. How much would the 4 additional ounces add to the cost? Well, if I divide the $3.49 price by 4, that would tell me the cost of 4 ounces. And dividing $3.49 by 4 is lots easier to do mentally that dividing $3.49 by 16. Let's see, $3.00 divided by 4 is $.75, and the extra $.49 is just a penny away from $.48, and $.48 divided by 4 is $.12. I add $.75 and $.12 and I get $.87. That's a quarter of a penny low, I realize, but close enough. Now I add $.87 to the 16-ounce price of $3.49. I can do that in my head. $3.49 and $.80 is $4.29, and $.07 more is $4.36. Aha! Even with the extra quarter-penny added on, the smaller container is a better buy by about 3 cents!

My friend Nicholas used a different approach. He figured out that the larger, 20-ounce container costs $.90 more than the smaller, 16-ounce container. "That's 4 more ounces for 90 cents," he told me, "which means that at that price 16 ounces would cost $3.60. But the 16-ounce container only cost $3.49, so it's a better buy." (You're probably wondering what kind of friends I have. Well, they're great friends—fun, caring, and as concerned about math phobia as I am.)

How come I didn't use either of these ways when I was in the drugstore? Well, I was rushed. Frazzled. Impatient. I wasn't in a good state of mind for thinking clearly about anything, mathematical or otherwise. But, with a little quiet time later, I figured it out on my own.

Afterward, it took some doing to follow Sandra's and Nicholas's approaches. But with some time and a bit of persistence, I saw how they reasoned. You may still be puzzled by their solutions. Remember, it's hard to follow someone else's reasoning.

There are some lessons here about solving math problems. Stay calm. Stick with it. Take your time. Ask friends for help. Think about how they reasoned to make sense of it for yourself. You'll be surprised how much you'll be able to do.

Problem 4
(from chapter 7)
Why does πr^2 make sense for figuring out the area of a circle?

The seventh graders were very curious about this formula for the area of a circle, and I tried to ease them into understanding it. I started by having them think about the formula for the area of a rectangle. That was easier for them and was useful for helping them make sense of πr^2. Try it.

Think about a rectangle that's 3 by 5 (inches, centimeters, feet, whatever).

You can find the area of a rectangle this size by multiplying its dimensions: 3 × 5 = 15. I've seen the formula for this written as $A = l \times w$ (length × width) or $A = b \times h$ (base × height). Either way, the area is 15 square units (square inches, square centimeters, square feet, etc.). You can check that by dividing the rectangle into squares and counting them.

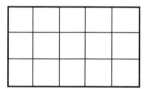

One more thing before getting to the circle. A square is a special rectangle because its sides are all the same length. To find the area of a square, since its length and width (or base and height) are both the same length, you multiply the length of a side by itself. So the area of a square that measures 3 of something on a side, for example, is 3 × 3, or 9 square somethings. Or we could write 3 × 3 as 3^2.

Okay, let's tackle circles. I'll close in on explaining why it makes sense that the area of a circle is equal to πr^2 by first presenting a way to explain why πr^2 is at least a reasonable ballpark figure. Remember that π is a little larger than 3 and r stands for the length of the radius of a circle, so according to the formula, the area of a circle is a little more than 3 times r times r.

Now think about a circle inscribed in a square. That means a circle drawn with a square around it like this:

The length of each side of the square is equal to the diameter of the circle. Since the diameter of a circle is twice its radius, it can be written mathematically as $2r$. So the length of each side of the square is equal to $2r$. To find the area of the square, you multiply the length of its side by itself. So the area of this square is $2r$ times $2r$, and that's the same as $4r^2$.

The formula for the area of a circle gives its area as πr^2, which is a little more than 3 times r^2. Since the circle is smaller than the square, it makes sense that its area is less than $4r^2$.

Now, suppose you were wondering about how to find the area of a parallelogram. (I know, I know, you weren't wondering any such thing. But play along.) A parallelogram is a four-sided shape, like a rectangle, but without necessarily having square corners. Here's what a parallelogram can look like.

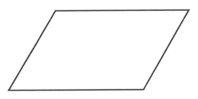

If you're wondering what a parallelogram has to do with understanding why the formula πr^2 produces the area of a circle, be patient. Please. One of the best ways to learn something new is to build on something you already know. I'm just rummaging around a bit to make sure you have a foundation on which I can build.

All right, the parallelogram. The formula for finding the area of a parallelogram is the same as the formula for finding the area of a rectangle. One way to see why this makes sense is by chopping a triangle off one side of the parallelogram and moving it to the other side. This changes the parallelogram into a rectangle, like this:

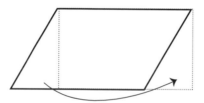

For a parallelogram, we use the formula $A = b \times h$, with b being the length of the base of the parallelogram and h the distance from the base to the top, which is the opposite side. (That's not the length of the slanty side; the slanty side is longer.)

Now, back to the circle. Imagine cutting a circle into eight segments, like slices of a pie:

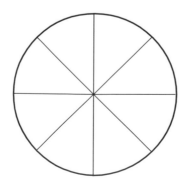

And imagine rearranging the slices into a curvy parallelogram-like shape, like this:

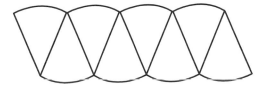

We can find the area of this parallelogram by multiplying its base by its height. Let's start with the base. It's the bumpy length at the bottom (or top) of this curvy parallelogram.

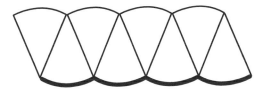

The bumpy top and bottom of the curvy parallelogram came from rearranging the circle's circumference. Half of the circumference makes up the base of the curvy parallelogram and the other half of the circumference makes up the top curvy side. So the length of the base is one-half of the circumference.

The full circumference of a circle is pi times its diameter (πd) or 2 times pi times the radius ($2\pi r$). (Look back in chapter 2 for an explanation of why this is so.) One-half of the circumference is half of $2\pi r$, which is πr, or π times the radius. So the two curvy sides—the base and the opposite side—are each πr.

Now we need to think about the height of the curvy parallelogram. The height is the same as the radius of the circle. Remember that the radius is the distance from the center of a circle to the edge. In a wedge of pie, you can draw the radius from the point of the slice to any point on its edge:

So the height of the curvy parallelogram is r.

To find the area of the curvy parallelogram, multiply its base (πr) times its height (r). That's πr times r. And r times r can be written as r^2, so the area of the curvy parallelogram is πr^2, which is how we figure the area of a circle.

Maybe you followed that, maybe you didn't. If you did, fine. If you didn't, I hope you're not feeling rotten about yourself—or hating me. Remember what I wrote at the beginning of this answer key about how hard it can be to follow someone else's reasoning. You have to turn the ideas around in your own head for yourself, I said, before you can make them your own.

If this explanation doesn't help, you may need to get paper and a pencil and make your own sketches. Or talk with a friend about this. Or put it aside and try again later.

Problem 5
(from chapter 7)

Imagine that you take a piece of string, wrap it around a Coke can, and cut it to that length. (The string would be the length of the circumference of the can.) Now imagine holding that string up to compare it with the height of the can. Would the string be shorter than the height of the can, taller, or about the same length? Why does this make mathematical sense?

It seems silly to give you the answer to this problem when you can find it out with a piece of string and a Coke can, verifying whether your answer is correct or not with some firsthand effort.

But I'll tell you anyway and then, if you like, you can check it out for yourself. The answer is that the string is taller than the height of the can. Quite a bit taller, actually.

This surprises most people. I think that's because it's difficult to visualize how long a circular distance will be when it's stretched out on a straightaway. But thinking about circles again can help.

The circumference of a circle is equal to π times its diameter. This is true for any circle, no matter its size. You may be sick of hearing about circles, but stick with me.

Hold your thumb and index finger the same distance apart as the diameter of the Coke can. The distance around the Coke can—the circumference of the circular top of the can, which is equal to πd, which is a little bit more than three times the diameter—is a little more than three times the distance between your thumb and index finger. And that's a good deal longer than the height of the can.

I've used this problem in many classes and talks that I've given to children and adults, and most people think that the distance around the Coke can is about the same as the height of the can. Also, most people remember learning about circles, though their memory of the formula $c = \pi d$ is generally dim or lost completely. That most people have forgotten the formula doesn't trouble me, because if you don't have a use for something, there's no reason to remember it. I've remembered it because I'm a math teacher.

However, when I was taught that formula, I learned it as a rule to follow, rather than as a relationship to understand. It's remarkable, I think, that for every circle, the relationship between the circumference and the diameter is the same, that the circumference of any circle is equal to a little more than three times its diameter. Maybe if more people understood that relationship, then more people wouldn't be fooled when they are presented with the Coke can question. And maybe if more people were taught to understand why the formula made sense, they would understand the relationship. Teaching for understanding isn't foolproof, but it's certainly a better approach.

Problem 6
(from chapter 10)
Why is $^{101}/_{201}$ greater than $^1/_2$?

This question is a candidate for the who-cares category of mathematical problems. Really, $^{101}/_{201}$ is awfully close to $^1/_2$, and who would care if it was a smidgen more or a smidgen less. Well, I can't think of a real-world reason that would call for thinking about that particular fraction. But let's give it a go.

In thinking about how we help children learn about fractions, $^{101}/_{201}$ can help us understand something about why children have difficulty understanding fractions and what we might do about it.

First the math. In order for a fraction to be equivalent to $^1/_2$, the numerator has to be exactly half of the denominator. No more, no less. If the numerator is greater than half the denominator, like $^2/_3$, then the fraction is greater than $^1/_2$. If the numerator is less than half the denominator, like $^1/_3$, then the fraction is less than $^1/_2$.

Half of 201 is $100^1/_2$; 101 is greater than $100^1/_2$; so $^{101}/_{201}$ is greater than $^1/_2$.

My friend Nicholas gave me another way to think about explaining this. (Remember Nicholas from the hand lotion problem?) He said to think about changing the denominator of $^{101}/_{201}$ so the fraction is $^{101}/_{202}$. That's exactly $^1/_2$ because 101 is half of 202. Now think of two pies each cut into equal-size slices. One is cut into 201 slices and the other is cut into 202 slices. The pieces from the pie cut into 202 slices will be smaller than the pieces from the pie cut into 201 slices. (I know, I know, this is silly. They'd be almost the same size. But thinking this way can get us somewhere here.) So . . . 101 pieces of the pie cut into 201 slices will be more pie than the 101 pieces of the pie cut into 202 slices. It will be a little more than half the pie.

While it's easy for most people to see that $^2/_3$ is greater than $^1/_2$ and $^1/_3$ is less than $^1/_2$, or even that $^8/_{15}$ is greater than $^1/_2$ and $^7/_{15}$ is less than $^1/_2$, it's more confusing to think about $^{101}/_{201}$. The numbers are larger and not as friendly. While it's easy to form a mental picture of $\frac{2}{3}$ or $\frac{1}{3}$, it's hard to form a mental picture of $\frac{101}{201}$ without analyzing the numbers.

I remember in school having to do fraction problems with unfriendly denominators, like adding $\frac{3}{4} + \frac{13}{15} + \frac{5}{6}$. In order to add, we had to change the fractions to equivalent fractions that had a common denominator, and we practiced the procedure for doing so on many examples. I never thought about estimating the answer first, to start by realizing that the answer had to be less than 3, but greater than 2, and maybe was about $2\frac{1}{2}$. I just plugged away at the problem using the procedure, my head in the trees, never thinking about the forest.

What's my point here? How does this relate to the $\frac{101}{201}$ question? I was never taught a rule for this sort of problem. I had to think about the meaning of the fraction in comparison to the meaning of $\frac{1}{2}$, not apply a procedure to crank out a response. But some people have learned only the rules, not the meaning, and get thrown when something calls for coloring outside of the lines of the procedures, even a little bit.

So it's true that $\frac{101}{201}$ is the kind of fraction most of us won't ever need to think much about. But it's also true that if we can't think about it and make sense of it, our mathematical power is far too limited. It's understanding that teaching should push for and nothing less.

Problem 7
(from chapter 11)
For discounted items, if the sales tax is figured on the original price first and then the discount is taken, would you pay more, less, or the same as if the sales tax had been figured on the discounted amount?

It doesn't matter to the customer. You pay the same either way.

You can see why this works if you take an example. Keep the numbers friendly. Suppose you buy something for $100 and suppose the discount is 10 percent and suppose the sales tax is 5 percent.

Way 1: Figure the sales tax on the regular price first and then take the discount. On $100, a 5 percent sales tax is $5 and that makes for a price of $105 with the tax. A 10 percent discount on $105 is $10.50, so the final price is $94.50.

Way 2: Figure the discount first and then the sales tax on the discounted amount. A 10 percent discount on $100 is $10, so the discounted price before tax is $90. The 5 percent sales tax on $90 is $4.50, so the total is $94.50.

For this example, the customer pays the same. But while it doesn't matter to the customer which way the amount is figured, the government may have a preference, since less tax is paid when it's figured the second way.

I hope you're convinced about this example. (Remember my earlier advice about having paper, pencil, and a calculator handy when you're reading mathematics. You might try this for yourself.)

But even if you're convinced that the amount paid is the same either way for this specific example, that doesn't necessarily prove that the amount will be the same if figured either way for all examples. You need to be able to generalize for all of the possible amounts, not draw a conclusion from one specific example, in order for a mathematical proof to be valid. And it's simply not possible to test this for every combination of amounts. You've got to rely on making a convincing argument.

Do you remember the commutative property for multiplication and the associative property for multiplication? The commutative property says that when you multiply two numbers, $a \times b$ gives the same result as $b \times a$, that the order doesn't matter. The associative property says that when you multiply three numbers— $a \times b \times c$—it doesn't matter if you multiply $a \times b$ first and then multiply the answer by c, or if you multiply $b \times c$ first and then multiply that result by a. You'll get the same answer either way.

When you figure the discount, you have to multiply. When you figure the sales tax, you have to multiply, and it doesn't matter if you do the discount multiplication first or the sales-tax multiplication first. It all comes out the same at the end, whatever the specific amounts.